T0351441

'The "Scandal" of Marxism'

THE FRENCH LIST

'The "Scandal" of Marxism'
and Other Writings
on **Politics**

Roland Barthes

Essays and Interviews,
Volume **2**

TRANSLATION AND
EDITORIAL COMMENTS
BY CHRIS TURNER

LONDON NEW YORK CALCUTTA

PAP
TAGORE
www.bibliofrance.in

The work is published with the support of the Publication Assistance
Programmes of the Institut français

Seagull Books, 2015

Compiled from Roland Barthes, *Oeuvres complètes* (Paris: Éditions du Seuil,
1993–2002).

© Éditions du Seuil, for *Oeuvres complètes, tome I*, 1993 and 2002

© Éditions du Seuil, for *Oeuvres complètes, tome II*, 1993, 1994 and 2002

© Éditions du Seuil, for *Oeuvres complètes, tome III*, 1994 and 2002

© Éditions du Seuil, for *Oeuvres complètes, tome IV*, 1994, 1995 and 2002

© Éditions du Seuil, for *Oeuvres complètes, tome V*, 1995 and 2002

English translations © Chris Turner, 2015

ISBN 978 0 8574 2 239 2

British Library Cataloguing-in-Publication Data
A catalogue record for this book is available from the British Library.

Book designed and typeset by Bishan Samaddar, Seagull Books, Calcutta, India
Printed and bound by Maple Press, York, Pennsylvania, USA

Contents

Do Revolutions Follow Laws?

Barthes's review of André Joussain's book *La Loi des révolutions* (Paris: Flammarion, 1950) for *Combat* on 20 July 1950 is his first published writing on the subject of history. *Combat* was a daily newspaper that developed out of the French Resistance's principal clandestine news-sheet. By 1950, when it was edited by the Warsaw-born Marxist Victor Fay, it was regarded as the main non-Communist newspaper of the radical Left. Barthes's earliest contacts with the paper were through Trotskyist literary critic Maurice Nadeau, to whom he had been introduced in 1947 by fellow sanatorium patient (and former concentration-camp inmate) Georges Fournié.

Nadeau was fulsome in his praise of his new collaborator at *Combat*, hailing him as a man with 'quelque chose de neuf à dire' [something new to say] (*Combat*, 1 August 1947). Barthes contributed several articles to *Combat* between that date and 1951, most of them book reviews (on Roger Caillois, Jean Cayrol and Michel Leiris, among others) or pieces that were later to be incorporated into the book *Le degré zero de l'écriture* (*Writing Degree Zero*. New York: Hill & Wang, 1968).

Oeuvres complètes, Volume 1, pp. 101–03

The philosophy of history is not by any means always in the service of history. This is because, by definition, it establishes a 'beyond' of history; it supposes laws, ends and a becoming [*devenir*] in history—things which separate from it to constitute an extra-historical site of reference, so that the history of human beings is replaced by the history of a destiny. And the philosophy of history doesn't need to avow a belief in any particular metaphysical or racist guiding principle to join the grand undertaking of the alienation of actual history in favour of some super-nature or other—a thing that has been pursued in various ways, though with increasing unease, since historical science itself acquired substance and solidity. It is enough merely for it to meditate 'scientifically' on the 'forms' of history to the detriment of its content.

This is what a philosopher—André Joussain—has just done by publishing a book entitled *La Loi des révolutions* [The Law of Revolutions], in which he attempts to classify the causes and the unfolding of a dozen revolutions in order to tease out a series of laws regarding their origins and development.

But, first, what is a revolution? For the author it seems that it is merely a change of regime and it doesn't matter to him whether it is accompanied by a shift in ownership or not. The seizure of power by Mussolini or by Hitler and Pétain's 'National Revolution' [*sic*] in 1940 are, it seems, revolutions just like the Russian revolution. It is very clear that such comparisons are possible only because the author views his revolutions from the greatest possible height—that is to say, from the most formal standpoint. As he sees it, the causes of revolutions divide up, for example, into psychological, social, permanent, periodic, intellectual, historical and so on. You would think you were reading a classification by Linnaeus. But just as in a Linnaeus plate there is always some scandalous animal that stands apart, such as the platypus, which, not having found its order or class, is discreetly ranged among the *paradoxa*, so M. Joussain's tables always contain, in the end, some solitary, inalienable, paradoxical event that defies all classification—namely, the revolution itself which, by its specific volume, exceeds the scholastic classifications into which it was to be splintered.

With his book, the author intends to lay the foundations of a new science, Comparative History. But that is much more of a Romantic idea, an idea of the kind that belongs to the beginnings of historical science when, unencumbered by documentary evidence and problems, it produced schemas and the kind of introductions, outlines and 'laws' that proliferated in the last century, from Herder to Hegel and from Montesquieu to Michelet. At that point, history had only one dimension: the philosophical. History today has several dimensions: the economic, the social, the intellectual, etc. The problem, then, is no longer to tease out laws, a mechanism or a 'thread', as they said at the time; it is to produce syntheses, as Henri Pirenne, Marc Bloch or Lucien Febvre strove to do.

Now, M. Joussain's revolutions are never syntheses; they are accumulations of causes, accidents and individualities, the variable mixture of which produces their diversity. Hence the postulate is once again presented that there are no differences in nature between the events of history; that revolutions are questions of degree; that historical facts can be freely handled, disembodied, taken apart and put back together again—in a word, alienated; that the essential substance of history no longer lies in time, within history and in men, but is outside time and place, outside history and in Man. For, as the author sees it, the law of revolutions lies, once and for all, in a human nature that is transcendent to history, which can be said to have its revolutions the way the body has its illnesses—revolutionary disturbances are simply the moments of an askesis which tends eventually towards the conservation of a past that is refreshed and restored to serenity by the relief at having survived a crisis and by the assurance that the masses, leaving the ordeal of anarchy behind, better understand 'the need for order and obedience' [*sic*]. For M. Joussain, revolutions are acts of hygiene or the enforcement of order.

In this way, under cover of comparative history, a systematic effort is made to downplay revolutions. Either the author equates them with mere political brigandage, picks them apart to produce a merely formal analysis, reduces them to a kind of gymnic askesis on the part of society or, lastly, subordinates them to the omnipotence of a Nature/Destiny/Providence whose role is to limit their effects to the minimum. For if that piece of trickery that is Man haunts the revolutions of M. Joussain, with his 'instincts' and his 'nature', actual men are absent from them. And yet we don't have the right to do these men out of this history—these men whose daily lives, wholly attached to a particular time, place and condition, have made history. We don't have the right to relate what determines the actions of a peasant in Luther's time to what drives a lawyer in the Constituent Assembly of 1789 or a worker in the Paris Commune. We don't have the right to substitute a general human mechanism for these specific figures, a mechanism whose revolutions would fall, more or less ripe, like fruits from a single tree.

Every historical fact, every historical human being is inalienable. And the law of revolutions belongs among the baggage of that ambiguous mythology which reasons about history only in order to spirit it away from the human beings who make it.

Combat (20 July 1950)

The 'Scandal'
of Marxism

The following article was published in *Combat* of 21 June 1951. Barthes was so exercised by Roger Caillois's book *Description du marxisme* (Paris: Gallimard, 1951) that he reviewed it twice—once for *Combat* and once for *Esprit* (see pp. *21–6*). Caillois, associated with Georges Bataille and Michel Leiris in the pre-war *Collège de Sociologie*, was by no means dismissive of the contributions of Marx and Engels to social science, but was critical of the way Marxism had become a rigid (Soviet) state doctrine. Caillois's critique took the rather oblique path of enquiring sociologically into the effects of Marxism in its actual functioning as a doctrinal *orthodoxy* ('My aim is to establish that an orthodoxy isn't an immutable truth, but a political truth—that is to say, a truth supported by a political power and subject to political obligations.'[1]) As readers will see, Barthes's initial response was that such a sociology was 'premature'.

Charles Guignebert, who is referred to in the second paragraph, was one of the

Oeuvres complètes,
Volume 1,
pp. 124–6

1 Caillois, *Description du marxisme*, p. 8.

first prominent secular historians of Christianity in France. A committed rationalist, he was critical of the tendency for religious dogma to insert itself into the history of the early Christian church and hence opposed to the histories of Christianity produced from an exclusively theological standpoint. He was also at odds with the 'modernists' within the Catholic church, whose project of doctrinal reform he regarded as contradictory.

Since it seems the Marxist 'church' has its orthodoxy, its schisms and its heresies, it must also have its sceptics and Pyrrhonians.

Roger Caillois would like to occupy that place, more or less as the Charles Guignebert of Marxism. Only, the critique of Christianity has always attacked the heart of the myth much more than its details. Caillois takes the opposite course: his 'description' of Marxism is concerned not with the idea—though he is rather scathing about it—but the reception it receives. Caillois observes Marxism at work in the modern world and finds a surprising mismatch between the flimsiness of the doctrine and the extent of its success. From this examination he derives a definition of orthodoxy—it isn't a timeless truth, but one that is political and subordinate to political requirements. In other words, Marxism derives its 'scandalous' prestige not from its own content but from the existence of the communist parties and Soviet Russia.

Caillois's description rests on a twofold movement: content and form, the doctrine and its orthodoxy discredit each other mutually. The doctrine, which is wrong in itself, has its mistaken nature magnified by the artificial nature of its success; and the success is itself scandalous because it represents the success of 'errors'. Thus it is not so important to judge the two terms in motion here—the doctrine and the myth—as to describe the relationship between them. Caillois is content, in fact, to condemn the doctrine in passing. The error would be no more significant than any other were it not exaggeratedly inflated; or, rather, the way Marxism is so puffed up when its object is actually so derisory represents a paradox defying all reason.

It is clear that ultimately, as Caillois sees it, the Marxist scandal is purely quantitative in nature. There must be something very reassuring about this finding for the opponents of Marxism—reduced to a quantity, the ideological power of communism happily has nothing disturbing to the reason about it. It is a merely phenomenal matter, as in the case of those monsters that are noteworthy solely by their disproportionate size—they are dangerous but not troubling. It was right, then, for Marxism's errors to be treated firmly and expeditiously. Otherwise, a discussion of ideas might have developed, and the sense of security bourgeois readers derive from the mathematical evidence of Marxism's outrageousness would have been disturbed. If Caillois dispatches the doctrine properly so-called in a few paragraphs, then that is because he has chosen his readers in advance—he doesn't have to convince, but only reassure, them.

There are, however, people in the world who retain a conception of Marxism that is just as unassailable by Muscovite dogmatism as it is by bourgeois scepticism. Their reply to Caillois would be that it isn't by any means immaterial whether Marxist orthodoxy rests on a handful of contemptible errors or a body of possible truths. In their eyes, Marxist dogmatism isn't the offensive paradox of a misbegotten theory elevated into *raison d'état*; it is the tragedy of a truth discredited by the weapons, beneath which it has been suffocated. For them, the scandal of Marxism isn't what separates error from triumph but what separates truth from its failure. And this is the nub—though the promotion of error is scandalous, the debasement of truth is tragic. Perhaps in the eyes of our bourgeois sceptics, contemporary Marxism is a paradox whose success brazenly offends against sound scientific logic. But for many dissidents, whose individual destinies continue to be enriched by Marxism, Muscovite dogmatism isn't a scandal—it is a tragedy, though in the midst of it they still try to retain, like the classical chorus, an awareness of misfortune, a sense of hope and a will to understand. For those people, Roger Caillois's description will seem like one of the many attempts at damping down the salutary unease which Marxism continues to inspire in the world, despite its zealots and its sceptics. They will consequently reject a method that seizes on the impostures of dogma to discredit once again the important things Marxism has to offer.

This is the problem—any sociology of Marxism is premature so long as the Marxist 'debate' itself is not exhausted by history. Yet this is far from being the case. We know that Marxist propositions at least represent active topics of discussion for the modern world; that those discussions are not as Byzantine as Caillois claims but relate in all cases to deep problems of current history; that we are not discussing the sex of angels but men's bread and butter; and that there is consequently a question prior to any 'situating' of the doctrine—namely, why or how Marxism is true or not.

Combat (21 June 1951)

Humanism without Words

***Oeuvres
complètes*,
Volume 1,
pp. 127–9**

In *Combat* of 30 August 1951, Barthes jointly reviewed Michel Leiris' 45-page UNESCO study *Race et civilisation* (subtitled *La question raciale devant la science moderne* [The Race Question in the Light of Modern Science]) and Daniel Guérin's book *Où va le peuple américain* (*Where is the American people heading?*), 2 vols (Paris: Julliard, 1950–51).

The writer and anthropologist Leiris (1901–90) was a member of the founding editorial team of *Les temps modernes* in 1945, and one of the major French intellectuals who helped the philosopher Alioune Diop to found and sustain the 'Pan-Africanist' journal *Présence africaine* in the same year. The ethnographer Alfred Métraux, whom Leiris cites in *Race et civilisation*, and Claude Lévi-Strauss (*Race et histoire*) also made significant contributions to UNESCO's antiracist campaign of 1951–52.

Daniel Guérin, the prominent Trotskyist, had lived in the USA from December 1946 to January 1949, where he became involved with the Civil Rights Movement. Part of *Où va le peuple américain* was translated into English as *Negroes on the March: A Frenchman's*

Report on the American Negro Struggle (New York, 1957). Guérin was denied re-entry to the USA in July 1950.

Racism isn't dead, it still has to be fought. How are we to do this? Apart from laws, the primary way is to explain it. In this connection, we would like to take as examples two recent texts which are limited in their aim and evince no particular ambition but which are noteworthy for the human value of their methods. One is a pamphlet by Michel Leiris, published by UNESCO, called *Race and Culture*. The other is the second volume of Daniel Guérin's work *Où va le peuple américain* [Where is the American people heading?], devoted largely to the race-relations problem [*le problème noir*]. Leiris simply reminds us of some purely common-sense facts that are so obvious as to be indisputable, except by passion and self-interest. He notes that racism doesn't only take violent and murderous forms—which still exist here and there even after the annihilation of Hitlerism—but has more diffuse manifestations also, such as the more or less general belief on the part of white people in the congenital superiority of their race. He denounces as fraudulent those who sought to underwrite racism with science and clarifies the common confusion between natural and cultural facts, between racial and social heritage. He sets out the limits of the notion of race, a notion distinct from culture, language and religion, confining it to a fact of physical anthropology, and in this way removes any value dimension from it. With the part played by nature reduced, that played by culture seems decisive: what racists attribute to race—qualities in their own case, failings in the case of others—belongs in reality to tradition or, in other words, to history. It is history which, to all intents and purposes, carries out the whole of the mental conditioning of human beings; it is history which produces the plurality of civilizations. It is, lastly, history which has, over the last hundred years or thereabouts and for very precise economic and political reasons, given rise to that racial prejudice which isn't an instinct but merely a cultural fact. So nothing lies outside history (except for a very few unimportant things, such as colour of skin or shape of face)—not even physical aptitudes, which have been shown by scientific testing to be the products of conditioning and history, not of nature. In this way, by means of his description of racism, Michel Leiris has succeeded in putting everything back in human hands: the disparity between civilizations and the fruitfulness of cultural contacts; the achievements of each culture and its qualities and failings; in short, the complexity of a history that leaves human beings both responsible for the evils they perpetrate and capable, in consequence, of remedying them.

Leiris shows the inanity of racial prejudice; Guérin, focusing on the particular problem of the American negroes, reveals its causes. These are exclusively historical and social—racial prejudice was developed and maintained to justify the exploitation of coloured people's labour [*la main-d'oeuvre de couleur*]. This means that it doesn't go back a long way—white racism, which emerged alongside modern capitalism and colonialism, is barely two centuries old; it reached its peak in the middle of the nineteenth century. In America, the largest wave of importation of slaves occurred between 1808 and 1860; at that date, there were four million slaves in the USA, as against 400,000 white slave-owners. This shows quite clearly that racism exactly followed the course of the development of American capitalism rather than correlating with democracy, that creed having been promulgated long before.

And it was because the condition of the black slave offended too flagrantly against the terms of that creed that the negro was really stripped of his quality as a human being and seen as a commodity. And in this way the contradiction disappeared, so capable has the bourgeoisie always been of lining up its interests, one way or another, with its sense of virtue. The whole of

Daniel Guérin's book issues from this explanation: the current condition of the American black [person], his attempts at liberation, his failures, the progress achieved and the route to an ultimate emancipation—all this is described effectively, once the facts have been taken out of the order of a false *nature* and put back into the true order of *history*.

Here again, as in Leiris, explanation isn't only the necessary form of truth but also the figure of hope. It is because nothing in the past exists outside of historical reason that the future can be wholly the property of the human beings who make it. The cultural explanation of allegedly natural facts is, therefore, a deeply humanistic move. It can even be said to represent the most concrete humanism, since hope here isn't a messianic postulate but a virtue of truth. At the same time, this hope contains its own weapons: with regard to a cultural fact like racial feeling, explanation is an authentic act of destruction—the first such act, if not the only one. The works by Michel Leiris and Daniel Guérin are perfect exemplars, then, of a specifically modern humanism, shorn of all verbal inflation and straightforwardly combining a concern for truth, a demand for justice and the ways to achieve these two things.

Combat (30 August 1951)

Phenomenology and Dialectical Materialism

The Hanoi-born philosopher and political activist Tran Duc Thao is still best remembered for his *Phénoménologie et matérialisme dialectique* (Paris: Éditions Minh-Tan, 1951), a book which is said to have fascinated such diverse philosophers as Louis Althusser, Jacques Derrida, Pierre Bourdieu and Paul Ricoeur. Paris was, at the time, in the grip of post-war existentialism, and efforts were being made in various quarters to ground a Marxist politics in phenomenology (not least, of course, by Jean-Paul Sartre). Tran Duc Thao took a less fashionable view, proposing that phenomenology could find a foundation in dialectical materialism, with the second part of his book devoted to the positing of a materialist genesis for human consciousness.

Barthes wrote this short and very positive review of the book for the 11 October 1951 edition of *Combat*.

Oeuvres complètes, Volume 1, pp. 130–1

Tran Duc Thao's book attempts to combine two methods which their proponents have until now believed do not mix: Husserl's phenomenology, and dialectical materialism. In combining them, Thao has not, strictly speaking, reconciled them with each other. What phenomenology can contribute to Marxism is a way of describing lived experience. It might be tempting to call this a language. What dialectical materialism contributes to phenomenological description, by contrast, is a horizon and a topping-off. The two stand, then, in a hierarchical relation, and Tran Duc Thao resolutely claims to be a Marxist—not a phenomenologist. Even when extensively clarified— something the author does throughout the first part of his book—phenomenology remains incomplete. Marxism, by contrast, is self-sufficient, and phenomenology merely acts as a kind of technical auxiliary. What we have here, in fact, is a progression. Phenomenology passes on the torch to Marxism and provides it with the actual vocabulary that enables it to describe the movement of consciousness and the myths of history.

Hence, in Part Two of his book, Tran Duc Thao uses phenomenological description to support two major contentions of Marxism. The first is that consciousness develops on the basis of matter. Here Tran Duc Thao analyses a range of animal and child behaviour and, describing the general discrepancy that exists between real acts and their lived meanings, is able to base any state of consciousness on a prior state of matter, since, as Thao understands it, 'There is nothing other in an intentional movement than a real movement that is half-made and then repressed.'[1]

The second Marxist proposition for which Thao mobilizes the phenomenological apparatus is that humanity's various ideologies each have a precise economic content. Thao establishes the dialectic of human societies, and shows in each mythology or philosophy the mimicked reflection of the economic relations of the moment.

Tran Duc Thao's quite brilliant demonstration has the immense virtue of bringing the evolution of ideas and myths back into the evolution of a deep history,

1 'I have preferred my own version here to the published English translation in which this passage is rendered as: 'The intentional movement is nothing other than a repressed outline of locomotion.' [Trans.]

which is the history of property or, more exactly, of the idea of ownership. No doubt the system of equations he provides does not entirely exhaust the countless mediations within history, but, such as it is, Thao's book represents the latest—though not the final—stage in reflective Marxism.

Combat (11 October 1951)

On a Metaphor.
(*Is Marxism a Church?*)

This second review of Caillois's *Description du marxisme* (Paris: Gallimard, 1951) was published in the literary/philosophical journal *Esprit*. Founded by Emmanuel Mounier in the spirit of 1930s Personalism, *Esprit* reopened at the Liberation with a more left-ward slant than it had shown before the war. By the time of this article (November 1951), its editorship had passed to the Swiss critic Albert Béguin, a close associate of Mounier and one who was, like him, committed to 'free, Christian thought'.

Oeuvres complètes, Volume 1, pp. 135–7

It has become almost a compulsory figure of speech to refer to the Marxist community as a Church. Roger Caillois did this again recently in his *Description du marxisme*. The metaphor originates with men who, being equally distrustful of Marxist and Christian ecumenisms, are intent upon gathering their opponents together under a single generic heading where they may mutually discredit one another. Whatever the motives for this, the metaphor implies a method. This consists in teasing out similar general characteristics from two different historical facts, setting up a sort of historical constant, and bringing Marxism and Christianity within the bounds of a purely institutional history that can be viewed in terms of a sociology of Forms. In this case, those common forms might be said to be hierarchy, dogmatism and infallibility. In this way, the Christian Church and Marxist society, divested of their causes, history and particular content, are reduced to the signs they may have in common.

Such a method probably dates from the nineteenth century. [René] Descartes and Voltaire had conceived of a history without order and connectedness, and hence without resemblance. With the Germans, the philosophy of history recovered the image, lost since Saint Augustine's day, of a homogeneous flow of historical time, a *sense* of history—that is to say, a direction in which it ran and a meaning for it. This conception required a methodological tool and that tool was analogy. What non-Cartesian philosophers or historians taught [Edgar] Quinet and [Jules] Michelet in the years around 1830 was to *construct* history by bringing together the similar elements. In this way, by a series of analogies, Michelet reconstituted the origins of Rome, inferring the unknown from the known. History found itself penetrated at this time by a host of themes, connecting distant points in time and introducing a soothing familiarity into the great mass of the past. The security thus generated was, as the historians of the time saw it, the security of science itself. Analogy was the scientific method par excellence, because nineteenth-century science, dominated as it was by the requirement for a Nature that was *composed* like a picture, could not be satisfied with a mere description of historical phenomena. It had, at all costs, to find their secret order and their engine—the reason, law, spirit or *organization* that underlay them—and it was at that time that this latter term first gained the prominence enjoyed ever since. Historical analogy corresponds to zoological transformism and chemical analysis—everywhere Nature, whether mineral, animal, human or historic, reveals itself to be bound and gathered within the limits of a continuous variation, within which characteristics echo one another. Formally—that is to say, essentially—the whole of Romantic thought from 1750 to 1850 rests in this way on the metaphor of the equational series or 'chain', an image which, combining both identity and variation of types, assumes that Nature possesses both continuity and 'becoming' [*devenir*].

Historical method found itself subject to a new exigency the day it was realized that the *characteristics* of a fact didn't absorb the whole of its content, that this latter was non-transferable, whereas the former could reproduce themselves from one fact to another. It became clear that history contained a contradictory assumption, for there is in it an irreversible movement and a stability of its general lines, an absolute disparity of content and a community of forms. The problem for modern historiography is how to account for both the structure and the flow of time; how to organize the past or, in other words, establish a relationship between facts that took place only once. Now, all scientistic history explains nothing, and all analogical history sacrifices the content of the fact. History is inalienable and yet it is explicable—this is the dilemma. Marx seems to have seen this—the class struggle, for example, isn't an analogy but an organizing principle, which in no way infringes upon the non-transferable content of each of its episodes; it is a constant coextensive with the singularity of the historical facts. However, instead of being a surface connection, analogy is set at the root of facts; we have here a hypo-phenomenon, so to speak, and in this way the order and movement of history are reconciled. Currently, the concerted development of the human sciences is gradually transforming the very notion of historical fact in such a way, for example, that a method of numerical analysis such as statistics can be applied to it. The modern historian's facts are gradually losing their individual character, and the dilemma of an ordered 'becoming' [*devenir*] of history is moving toward a resolution. We are on the way to a new conception of history, in which it will be a science of the irreversible and yet also of the repeated.

Comparison of the characteristics shared by the Christian Church and Marxist society is clearly not part of that history. What we have there is a surface similarity, partial effects, spectacular but limited epiphenomena that are the products, in the best of cases, of the old analogical method. It is insofar as the Marxist church metaphor implies a standpoint external to the Church and to Marxism, and assumes the air of disinterested objectivity that it represents an imposture. For the objectivity is contentless; it explains nothing, establishes no connections and fails to get beyond the merely emotive level; it remains a rhetorical objectivity. One is clearly entitled to use it, if one wants. But in what interests? To convince whom? And to establish what truth?

P.S. This church mania is decidedly all the rage. The bishop of Bayonne has just called, in connection with school subsidies, for the disestablishment of the 'secular Church'. There is some piquancy in seeing the word 'Church' at last become a pejorative term in the hands of a bishop. All paradox apart, this is another one to add to the list of false metaphors and illusory comparisons, which, like all the undiagnosed disorders of language, debase human relations.

Esprit (November 1951)

Left–Wing Writers
or Left–Wing Literature?

When Henri Smadja became the sole director of *Combat* in 1951, he moved the newspaper sharply to the political Right. At that point Claude Bourdet invited Maurice Nadeau to join him at *L'Observateur* and run the weekly magazine's literary supplement. Barthes, who had just returned from a period as a French *lecteur* in Alexandria, wrote to Nadeau to say that he would like to be able 'to work again for you and with you' and Nadeau subsequently invited him to produce articles for both *L'Observateur* and, more frequently, *Les Lettres nouvelles*. This questionnaire and article, published in *L'Observateur* on 27 November 1952, were part of an effort to survey the magazine's readership on the question of 'left-wing literature'.

Oeuvres complètes, Volume 1, pp. 163–5

1. *Is it currently possible to define a left-wing literature?*
2. *Is that left-wing literature defined by a content that is its own and lends it its unity?*
3. *From the standpoint of 'literary art', can a work exclude itself from the Left by its form?*
4. *Must a left-wing work necessarily be addressed to the masses? Is a work that reaches the masses necessarily left-wing?*
5. *Is a left-wing work fated to have only an immediate combative value or can it in fact be left-wing over a number of generations?*

   A sixth question is addressed individually to each of the writers surveyed.

Before even defining two words as vital and as confused as 'literature' and 'Left', it is clear to me that *left-wing literature* has a reality coextensive with all these definitions and that it is, before we even discuss its content, a meeting place, the starting point for a struggle, and a—more or less activist—gathering of all the writers who profess a left-wing politics. I am able, then, to give at least an immediate definition of left-wing literature: *It is the production of left-wing writers.* I am unable, without analysis or discussion, to grasp the ideological content of the novels of [Louis] Aragon or Sartre, and yet I know right away that they are part of a left-wing literature, because the one is a communist and the other has taken a public stand in favour of the proletariat and against racism, and all their works are condemned by the Church of the bishops and by the representatives of Capital.

Left-wing literature has, therefore, a power that is prior or superior or external—however one chooses to see it—to its content; like all effective words, it possesses a sort of power of intimidation. Whatever its reality, it is a salutary myth, insofar as it helps to bring people together, draws the battle lines, unifies the forces and gives a name to the struggle. But there comes a point, all the same, when this reassuring expression has to be given an in-depth, rather than merely a broad, definition—when we have to go beyond its power of intimidation to its power of definition. It is here, then, that our investigation must begin, at this point where left-wing writers—defined and united by the opinions they profess, the slogans they defend, the manifestos they sign, the congresses they attend and the magazines in which they write— *step aside to reveal their productions*; the point where their own selves fall silent, ceding the stage to literature in all its solitude and mystery, which now stands before us beneath the true gaze of history.

What, then, is left-wing literature? Is it not something less extensive and more profound than what left-wing writers produce? Is there a common thematics to all these left-wing works? Do they all have the same concerns with form, with audience, with longevity? Do they have meaning in the here-and-now or on a historical scale? Is the USSR right, for example, to regard [Honoré de] Balzac, a Catholic and a monarchist, as a progressive author? How is it that the left-wing press of his day judged [Émile] Zola's work reactionary before he intervened in the Dreyfus Affair?

These last questions relate to the past, but are not perhaps without interest insofar as they rightly make definitions dependent on historical explanation. Let us attempt that explanation, not to bend the investigation in a particular direction but to indicate its limits. We know that, up until the triumph of modern capitalism, the left-wing artwork always remained *internal to bourgeois ideology*; it was sufficient to believe in the bourgeois progress of society, in a universal spread of the bourgeois essence, in the bourgeoisie itself producing beneficial—bourgeois—effects. But with the coming of the last stage of capitalism, the universal dream of the liberal bourgeoisie vanished in the harsh light of class differences; the proletariat entered the bourgeois consciousness as a kind of unavoidable outrage; the left-wing writer, peaceably striving up to that point to clarify an essentialist view of man that came straight from the eighteenth century, found himself struck by the rivenness of society and in constant restless movement; he was increasingly defined by *the untenable character of his situation*, caught as he was between a detested origin and an unattainable end-goal.

This explains why in the nineteenth century, up to the Dreyfus Affair, left-wing writers defined themselves primarily by *what they wrote*, and why today they define themselves primarily by *who they are*. Ask whether Michelet was on the Left and no one will tell you he was a liberal candidate in the legislative elections and removed from his public functions by Napoleon III, but everyone knows that the whole of his works assert the historical struggle and the rise of the people. Ask the same question about a contemporary author and you will most often find that the writings are merely a kind of opaque preliminary that complements the resounding commitment of the person—the work lays the ground for the commitment, it does not contain it.

Can it still contain it? The aim here isn't to take an inventory of opinions but to elicit explanations. The survey proposed here has nothing of the Gallup poll about it: it is a genuine questioning, coming at a moment when literature is almost entirely recognized *as a site of responsibility* and when, in the eyes of many writers—including some of the best—political commitment represents a veritable exculpation of literature. We shall know more about this—both about literature and about the Left—when we are able to explain why a writer may be on the Left otherwise than by saying so.

L'Observateur (27 November 1952)

Yes, There Definitely Is a Left-Wing Literature

This article, originally published in *L'Obser-vateur* of 15 January 1953, summarizes the responses to the questionnaire of the previous section. It was co-written with Maurice Nadeau.

Oeuvres complètes, Volume 1, pp. 229–33

We realize, from the number and the quality of the responses we have received, that the debate we sought to initiate between a number of writers and our readers on 'literature and the Left' was complex and difficult. It is based, in fact, on some vague, traditionally accepted notions that were in need of redefinition. What is the Left? What is a left-wing literature? Is it enough to describe oneself as being on the Left to produce left-wing works? What is literature, even? These are the questions our correspondents have generally considered.

*

Though our initial hypothesis—that we distinguish the left-wing writer, defined by the hostile reactions of the clerical and bourgeois world, from left-wing writing, for which we were precisely seeking a definition—has met with general acceptance, it has nonetheless been contested to some degree.

34

For example, André Bay, the champion of a pure literature free from all social and political contingencies, refuses to confuse the non-conformism, which is, in his view, manifested by any literary work, with the Left, which he regards merely as the relic of a dead humanism. But doesn't he himself create the confusion he accuses us of perpetuating when he lumps all literary writers together in the same non-conformist bag? Is it enough merely to pick up a pen to become immediately—and, apparently, without deliberate intent—a scourge of the values of the age? If all literature is left-wing by definition, it is indeed useless to attach a label to it. Or we shall have to deny the name of 'writer' to fascist or collaborationist writers and, indeed, to all those who defend established values—something which, despite our 'leftism', we refuse to do.

André Dhôtel, who also situates literature firmly outside the political and social spheres, stays closer to the sources of the literary phenomenon when he characterizes it as 'an astonishment' at the world—an astonishment that it is literature's calling to express. There is, as he sees it, a 'secret history' of human beings and their lives that alone belongs to the field of literature. Why this amputation? And why would the 'overt' history of human beings not also provide subject matter for description, reflection and expression? Is it not the attitude of the writer to this overt history, his desire to find its meaning or to give it one, that show him as belonging 'on the right' or 'on the left', among the upholders of a certain order or its denigrators, among the conservatives or the progressives? Is it true that, 'the Blacks, the *poètes maudits* and the literary daredevils who never get a mention' fall outside 'the general categories of literature or history'? Are they not in general the victims of that history? Isn't their work a protest against a denial of social or individual justice? Is it not from an awareness of that denied justice that they derive the form of their anathemas or their calls for 'another kind of life'?

*

In contrast to the supporters of a literature without labels, a number of our correspondents advocate a literature in the service of a philosophy, an ethic or a politics. Since revolution is necessary and written into the fabric of things, all the efforts of those who call for it and are preparing for it, men of letters included, must converge towards the same end. The progressive or revolutionary writer is an activist of a certain kind, specializing in a particular sort of work, who must, in his own way, clearly show that he stands on the side of progress and the future. For example, this is what M. Desgriffes from Marcinelle (Belgium) tells us: 'For freedom, against serfdom and oppression, for socialism against oppression, the men and women of today are engaged in a ruthless struggle. Only the literature that gives genuine support to that struggle is valid.' M. Exquerra, a lawyer at Toulouse, is even more precise: 'If the path of social progress necessarily involves the

Communist Party becoming the leading political force in France, literature oriented in the opposite direction is a reactionary literature, a right-wing literature.'

One can see what is so seductive and so impossible about this point of view. On the one hand, it establishes a clear classification; on the other, it denies literature, for would this not be a 'literature' with no other function than to amplify slogans, illustrate them and, in the end, justify them, transitory as they might be? In that sphere, political activists are better writers than writers themselves and render literature useless, if not indeed harmful. Literature, for its part, will always lag behind slogans and will always create confusion around what is, by definition, clear and final.

We should, in fact, point out that this is a consumer's viewpoint. The producer or, in other words, the writer, even if he is a communist, is not willing to go that far. He makes a point of declaring that he doesn't, in any way, follow orders and that he is 'free'. His works are the product of a fortunate encounter between what the activists in his party think and what he thinks himself, so much is it the case—as most of our correspondents assert—that literary creation, if it is to exist at all, requires the total independence of the writer. It is not true, M. Jean Guilhem at Cahors tells us, that 'the more one campaigns, the better one writes'; in a field of this kind, it all depends on the individual and the subject.

*

Between these two contradictory positions, which reject the existence of a left-wing literature in favour of either a literature without labels or a party literature, stand all those—and they are the majority—who strive to define the content of a left-wing work independently of its form and intention. As we have seen, the example of Balzac recurs rather frequently, as even do 'obsequious government lackeys' (Edgar Morin), whose contributions have come, over time, to be 'progressive', despite their intentions. Left-wing literature has certain markers of identity. They might be formulated as follows:

1. Literature isn't a thing but a relation, a 'mediation' between man and the world (Edgar Morin). The reactionary or totalitarian work is recognizable by the way it destroys this living relation and makes a fetish of the work. By contrast, Left, progressive or revolutionary literature is movement, surpassing, questioning. Far from attempting to set itself up as something timeless or eternal, it knows that it is mortal and may go so far as to problematize itself.

2. Left-wing literature is a literature of troubled concern and rejection. Its attitude is non-conformist and heretical towards all orthodoxies, even left-wing ones. It criticizes the values of the bourgeois order, campaigns in favour of minorities, protests constantly against injustice, and argues overtly or covertly for the coming of a new man within a just society (the responses of Francis Jourdain, Michelle

Esday, Henri Féraud, Jean Cordelier and Jean Guilhem who says very rightly that 'left-wing literature will always be at odds with orthodoxy. Its aim is to raise problems, to prevent torpor and sclerosis').

3. Left-wing literature is a literature that fights against all violations of the irrepressible right to life (David Rousset, Michelle Esday, Jean Cordelier).

4. Left-wing literature gives a new meaning to the word 'humanism'—in whose name all the abuses of human beings are perpetrated—by making it synonymous with a liberation of human beings by themselves, without any metaphysical or religious adjunct. There may be left-wing Catholic or Protestant authors, but a literature cannot call itself left wing if, for the problems it raises, it provides a pre-established solution that is valid once and for all.

5. In the last instance, the left-wing work of literature is always a description and a deep analysis of a given historical situation, even if it confines itself to the sphere of the individual. It situates the individual in his milieu, his social group, the form of society to which he belongs, failing which his feelings, thoughts and behaviour would be incomprehensible. It isn't necessary for this sociological environment itself to be described. It is enough that it is hinted at. [Marcel] Proust's work, offered as a rather unexpected example by Edgar Morin

and Francis Jourdain, is progressive insofar as, being concerned to depict individuals, Proust has succeeded in dissecting the behaviour of an entire social group without resorting to idealist explanations. By *simultaneously lifting the veil on* historical *and* eternal man, left-wing literature contributes to a kind of sociological elucidation of the various moments of a collective history of humanity (Edgar Morin, Francis Jourdain, Michelle Esday, together with M. Desgriffes at Marcinelle and M. Ebely at Montgeron).

*

We may ask, by way of a counter-argument, whether literature as a whole doesn't possess the characteristics we have just specified. We have to reply in the negative. Whether used merely as a means (as a source of income, an ideological vehicle or to entertain a particular audience) or, by its worthiest producers, as an end, it often oscillates between commercial activity and aesthetics. It isn't enough to speak of the independence and freedom of writers or their rejection of formal commitments. There are entirely independent writers who have nothing to express but trivialities and even more of them know nothing of the age they live in. The path of a left-wing literature runs towards greater awareness, on the one hand, and greater mastery, on the other. It starts out from the probity of the artist and ends in the truth of what he expresses. In a world of permanent, many-sided mystification, the left-wing work deflates myths, exposes deception and tirelessly bears witness to the fact that human ills need remedying. It bears the marks of clear-sightedness and courage.

A combative literature? Without doubt it is. But its combat isn't only over the questions eternal man asks himself, but also those of historical man. The writer isn't fighting for a change of government, even if such a change were highly desirable, but a transformation of the conditions, both external and internal, that determine individuals, their thinking and their morality.

Does it thereby go beyond the field of literature? Quite possibly it does, and, in that sense, Edgar Morin is right to say that the 'left-wing' character of a literary work is its 'accursed part, the dissatisfaction out of which it arises, the political demand [*revendication*] it implies.' It is also its living part, without which it would sink into mere entertainment, triviality and support for the established order. We may even say that left-wing literature bolsters and develops within itself all that isn't literature; that it aims for that ultimate point where literature would be merely the ritual *form* of its own self-questioning and a direct passage from the field of expression into the real world of history. If that moment ever comes, it is possible that literature will die. But that is because it will have transformed itself into history.

L'Observateur (15 January 1953)

The Masters and the Slaves

***Oeuvres complètes,* Volume 1, pp. 253–4**

This review of Gilberto Freyre's *The Masters and the Slaves: A Study in the Development of Brazilian Civilization* (New York: Alfred A. Knopf, 1964) appeared in the first issue of *Les Lettres nouvelles* in March 1953. Barthes also contributed a review of Jean Vilar's staging of Heinrich Kleist's *Prinz Friedrich von Homburg* at the Théâtre National Populaire to this same issue of the magazine which Maurice Nadeau had founded with Maurice Saillet.

The Portuguese original of Freyre's book, entitled *Casa-Grande & Senzala*, was first published in 1933. It was translated into French, as *Maîtres et esclaves, la formation de la société brésilienne*, by the eminent sociologist Roger Bastide.

Just imagine that only three or four centuries after the last Frankish invasions, some historical scholar, miraculously equipped with all the powers of modern science, had produced a work of synthesis on the ethnic formation of the French people. It is easy then to see how prodigiously interesting for us as Frenchmen an analysis shaped by the most recent methods of anthropology, dietetics or psychoanalysis would be, when applied to ethnic facts that went back only a few generations.

The combination of a still very recent racial history with a great mind nourished on the most advanced disciplines has provided Brazil with just such a prestigious work. Gilberto Freyre's *The Masters and the Slaves* (the title is almost too Hegelian for a content that is, all things considered, materialist) takes as its subject the ethnic mix of Portuguese, Indians and Negroes in Brazil. The phenomenon is treated in all its aspects—historical, economic, religious, ethnic, sexual, culinary, moral, etc.—and by all currently available methods:

social history, anthropology, human geography, dietetics, psychoanalysis, etc. The book is a brilliant product of that sensitivity to total history developed in France by historians like Marc Bloch, Lucien Febvre and Fernand Braudel.

The Masters and the Slaves commands admiration. It is an exceptional work from many points of view. While being as broadly insightful as the writings of a Marc Bloch or a Lucien Febvre, it has also that accidental quality we have just pointed out, in that the historical subject matter it has to systematize has barely yet flown free of the human body, of health, of diet, of the phenomenon of the mixing of blood and humours. The historians' squaring of the circle is almost achieved here, the *summum* of historical research in the view of men like Michelet or Bloch. It is all done with the brio of a Keyserling, but the difference between the two is one of truth: Freyre's book is explosively laden with concrete facts and his grasp of them goes far beyond the written document or the tourist observation within a Brazilian ecology still wholly dominated by the proximity of its ethnic prehistory. There is, moreover, in Freyre an obsessive sense of substance, of tangible matter, of the object, so to speak, which is ultimately the specific quality of all the great historians.

Lastly, Freyre is an innovator—he has introduced a sexology conceived on the historical scale into the history of the Brazilians, both by explaining the Brazilian's open sexuality and his taste for heterogeneous unions in terms of the genuinely Freudian relations of the young white child with his black nurse, and by describing the equilibrium historically established between the sort of satyriasis of the Portuguese conquerors and the relatively weak sexual tonus (contrary to the prevailing prejudice) of the aboriginal Indians and the black people imported from Africa. We find this sort of determinism convincing because it is always located in a well-defined historical and social situation (the agrarian, slave-owning structure of early Brazilian society, the first 'liberal' directives of the missionaries, etc.).

Lastly, if one calls to mind the horrendous mystification that the concept of race has always represented, and the lies and crimes the word continues to underwrite in various places, it will be recognized that this intelligent, scientific book is also a work of courage and struggle. To introduce explanation into myth is, for the intellectual, the only effective form of political activism.

Les Lettres nouvelles (March 1953)

Am I a Marxist?

Oeuvres complètes, Volume 1, p. 596

In February 1955, Barthes published a review of Albert Camus's 1947 novel *La Peste* [The Plague] in the magazine *Club*, criticizing its symbolism and consequent lack of 'considered political content'. Replying to Barthes's criticism, Camus asked in the name of what higher morality the critic rejected the explicit morality of his novel. Barthes replied that he took his stand on the ground of 'historical materialism', and went on to say that he 'regard[ed] a morality of explanation as more complete than a morality of expression' ('Réponse de Roland Barthes à Albert Camus', *Club*, April 1955).

In the same month, Barthes was challenged by Jean Guérin in the *Nouvelle nouvelle revue française*[1] to explain, with regard to his series of 'Mythologies' articles, whether there was anything that didn't count for him as

---

1 The *Nouvelle revue française* was banned at the Liberation for its collaboration, under the direction of Pierre Drieu la Rochelle, with the occupying Nazi authorities. Hence, when it recommenced publication in 1953, it did so as *La nouvelle nouvelle revue française*, though it reverted to the old title after 1958.

a 'myth'. Barthes published the following reply in *Les Lettres nouvelles* of July–August 1955.

Quoting some extracts from these 'Mythologies'[2] in the June issue of the *Nouvelle nouvelle revue française*, M. Jean Guérin enjoins me to say whether I am a Marxist or not.[3]

Ultimately, what concern is that of M. Guérin's? These kind of questions are normally of interest only to McCarthyites. Others still prefer to judge by the evidence. M. Guérin would be better advised to do as they do. Let him read Marx, for example.

There he will discover—at least I hope he will—that you don't become a Marxist by immersion, initiation or self-proclamation, the way you become a Baptist, a Trobriand islander or a Mohammedan; that Marxism isn't a religion but a method of explanation and action; that that method demands a great deal of those

---

2 Barthes's 'Mythologies' pieces were initially published in *Les Lettres nouvelles*, under the editorship of Maurice Nadeau. [Trans.]

3 '. . . But, after all, perhaps M. Roland Barthes is simply a Marxist. Why does he not say so?'

who claim to practice it; and that, as a result, calling oneself a Marxist is more about self-importance than simplicity.

I appreciate that it would be so much more reassuring if we could divide up writers in terms of their 'simple' declarations of faith, leaving it possible then to claim the prestige of 'freedom' for those who didn't have one.

It would be more reassuring but less rigorous. Where Literature is concerned, reading is a more objective method than an opinion survey. I have only to read the *Nouvelle Nouvelle Revue Française*, for example, to recognize its entirely reactionary character; I have no need of any declaration on the subject.

Les Lettres nouvelles (July–August 1955)

Is Anti-Semitism
Right– or Left–Wing?

This brief text was Barthes's response to a survey of November 1958 conducted by the Jewish monthly magazine *L'Arche*, which was founded in 1957 by the Fonds social juif unifié [Unified Jewish Social Fund].

The Lacoste referred to in the first paragraph is Robert Lacoste, Governor General of Algeria under Guy Mollet's Socialist government of February 1956–May 1958.

Oeuvres complètes, Volume 1, pp. 933–4

We have known for a long time that Right and Left are confused notions. They can each be led, for tactical reasons, to exchange their positions (Lacoste has carried out a right-wing policy in Algeria and there is, conversely, a right-wing anti-colonialism). Socially, all classes are capable at some time of shifting politically and even of dividing (as is probably the case with the working class, which has just voted partly 'yes' and partly 'no' at the last referendum). Lastly, to make the confusion complete, in our present-day world—and peculiarly in France—the Communist Party renders the notion of the Left terribly ambiguous at the moment.

There remains the ideological criterion. By ideology is to be understood a general representation of the world, the political determinations of which (in the broad sense of the term) are generally unconscious. Right-wing ideology is defined by a certain number of beliefs which, taken together, form a sensibility: rejection of history; belief in a changeless human nature; more or less explicit recognition of force as a value; anti-intellectualism, etc.

The definition of the Right depends on these elements being brought together—not the other way about. Since anti-Semitism is one of them—and not the least significant—it follows that *it is anti-Semitism that makes the Right, not the Right that makes anti-Semitism.* Anyone who is anti-Semitic defines himself as a rightist and thereby defines the Right. We should go further here—someone who announced he was a man of the Left but professed anti-Semitism would unmask himself by so doing as following a right-wing ideology: anti-Semites are always right-wingers, right-wingers are not necessarily anti-Semites.

Of course there is a significant affinity between the implicit assumption of racism (refusal to recognize the other) and the Right's ideological immobilism, its egocentrism, its violent rejection of all behaviours of otherness, its connivance in cultivating identity, in being comfortable only with its own kind, in considering others as congenitally alien. But among some right-wingers, liberalism may temper this kind of narcissism.

L'Arche (November 1958)

Home
Knitting

Oeuvres complètes, Volume 1, pp. 963–6

This article, published in *Les Lettres nouvelles* of 1 April 1959, is a further example of Barthes's 'Mythologies', though one possessing a particularly urgent political quality. The uprising against French colonial rule that was launched by the FLN (National Liberation Front) on 1 November 1954, quickly developed into a war of independence and this 'Algerian War' (1954–62) dominated French politics dramatically for much of the next decade, causing the overthrow of the French Fourth Republic in May 1958 and its replacement by a Fifth Republic with a strong presidential role specifically designed for the 'providential' figure of de Gaulle.

General Jacques Émile Massu, commander of the *groupe parachutiste d'intervention*, emerged victorious from the 'Battle of Algiers' in October 1957, defeating and capturing the leadership of the FLN by a counter-insurgency strategy based on the widespread use of torture. During the Algiers crisis of May 1958, when it became clear that the government had decided to negotiate with the Algerian nationalists, rightist elements organized by former Governor General Jacques Soustelle and led by General

Massu seized power in Algiers and threatened to move to overthrow the French government, using paratroopers and other armoured forces, unless de Gaulle were made head of state. In the end, the Fourth Republic fell to a bloodless coup when de Gaulle was made 'président du conseil', empowered to rule by decree and authorized to initiate constitutional change. After elections in November 1958, de Gaulle became the first president of the Fifth Republic. He was subsequently to outmanoeuvre the pro-colonial rightists who had played such a part in bringing him to power, removing General Massu from his Algerian post in January 1960 on the pretext of a provocative interview the general had given to the *Süddeutsche Zeitung*, and eventually granting Algeria its independence.

In a usage that perhaps seem strange to English-speakers, the wives of French generals are accorded the courtesy title *Madame la Générale*. Given the rather ironic use Barthes makes of this, I have retained the term in French in the translation. The word *fellagha*, which will also be unfamiliar to many readers, refers to the guerrilla soldiers fighting for national independence. It derives from an Arabic word meaning bandit.

Aux Écoutes was a weekly magazine which ceased publication in 1969. It was right wing in political tendency and is perhaps best known for publishing the caricatures of Jean Sennep.

As the founder of the Maison du Soldat, an employment agency and the organization *Tricots à domicile* (Home Knitting), the wife of General Massu battles unstintingly on the social front. As we learn from the *Aux écoutes* magazine of 13 March 1959, her HQ in the rue d'Isly in Algiers is as bare as a warrior's tent. Its stark emptiness is a standing rebuke to the Civil Service with its piles of paperwork and red tape. Most importantly, however, like those great scientists who reduce the universe to a few equations with a simple piece of chalk or the real rulers of the world who do their thinking at an empty desk, Madame la Générale is telling us, with the choice of this austere decor, that the mere tools of action are a mundane matter, that only the brain has value, that deep thought is intangible, and that a great captain, like the great doctor doing his rounds without his white coat or the great teacher delivering his lesson without notes, may dispense with the marks of his office. In short, she is saying that the only matter worthy of the genius is abstraction—the bareness of the premises ensures that what is dealt with in them is essential.

In this rarefied, anonymous space, two objects alone connect the general's wife to the world, like the two ends of a circuit in which she is a humble relay. These are a number of close-up shots of General Massu in his parachutist's uniform—no doubt a source of inspiration to her—and, at the other end of the scale—and as markers of the thoroughly down-to-earth reality that has to be shaken up and transformed—two telephones that are constantly ringing, keeping Mme la Générale informed minute by minute of the successive skirmishes in the Knitting War. For this almost abstract place is also everywhere at once—everything converges here and everything emanates from here too, a single source of thought producing multiple effects since there are *two* telephones. Like every great strategist, Mme la Générale *faces down her enemies* (we are told). She keeps up a battle on several fronts—here, the defeatist press, there the *fellagha*. Hence the range of her weapons—yesterday sewing machines, today home knitting. Yet there is a great overarching political philosophy behind this entirely contingent activity. The good soldier knows how to win. The great captain does even better—he takes a stand on the essence of things. The philosophy of General Massu's wife is staunchly nominalist. When will the Algerian war end? *The day people in France stop saying there is a chance that it will not end well.* All in all, things exist only because they are named. Following the time-honoured magic, then, to eliminate the name is to eliminate the thing. Mme la Générale dreams of a great silent France where the talk will be only of knitting.

Most importantly, General Massu's wife has the key attribute of the great captain—*a smiling serenity.* How many things are conveyed by this calm Soldier's smile! The certainty of the Cause and the exemplary nature of its methods; the superhuman quality of one who remains in control of herself and the universe despite the two simultaneous telephones; a certain 'detachment' from earthly concerns, discreetly reflecting privileged lines of communication with the gods and an airy sense that the Knitting Front is, after all, a mere *worldly concern*; the magnanimous indulgence of a merely human agitation in which one participates only to raise it to a higher level; the relinquishment of all hatred, the serenity of the Stoic; and lastly, perhaps, and most importantly, the privilege of the female sex, called to light up with a smile the hard battles fought by men, overgrown children that they are. Like a somewhat sibylline Olympian goddess, Mme la Générale imparts to her serene smile the wisdom of *the one who knows all* but does not tell, for to smile is always to say less than one might.

It should be said that she does implicitly acknowledge that everything isn't going swimmingly in Algeria. Were that not the case, would she have founded *Tricots à domicile*? But the trouble is limited in nature and we shall shortly see its cause: for Muslim women, it lies in a mild degree of poverty, combined with a great lack of useful work, since 15,000 francs a month for home-working (the income provided by *Tricots à domicile*) will remedy it. In this way, dividing the task between them sensibly, the General and his wife are able to take care of the complementary aspects of the Algerian 'problem': as a man, the General is fighting the war and overcoming the *fellagha*; as a woman, his wife is reconstructing, and rallying the female population by sending them to their knitting needles.

Here two themes of differing origins are mingled. The first, the theme of homeworking, represents one of the most outdated forms of capitalist alienation: General Massu's wife's programme dates more or less from the Restoration (1814–30). But most impor-tantly—and to stay within the limits of mythological analysis—this form of wage-lábour has a triple morality to it. First, by turning the labour into craftwork, it becomes possible to lend it a spirituality, to set off the *enriching* virtues of natural labour with its quasi-biblical characteristics against the inhumanity of the factory. Second, working at home keeps husband and wife together; it pretends to emancipate the wife, and to grant her the male privilege of earning without actu-ally taking her away from her pots and pans and her washing—in a word, away from what is nobly termed the 'hearth and home'. Lastly, in accordance with the basic sophistry of bourgeois ideology, charity cleverly becomes the driver of work; you can save your soul and rescue the laws of the economy at one and the same time. The charitable aspect sublimates the element of labour, while the labour involved rehabilitates the charitable element—killing two birds with one stone is, after all, the golden rule of an accounting-based civilization. *Aux écoutes* is only too happy to break this revolving mechanism down into its two parts: 'As the Battle of Algiers was raging', Monseigneur Duval's vicar brought General Massu's wife a suitcase containing 50 million francs from an anonymous penitent (unlikely to be one of the *fellagha*) and the journalist is not slow to connect this staggering donation with the philanthropic organizations Mme la Générale has created, as though it followed inevitably—from charity to employment agency, the path is straight and smooth.

The second theme that looms behind Mme Massu's *organization* is that of the Muslim woman. This Muslim woman, who has been presented as something of a puzzle to us since 13 May, being always filmed veiled but voting determinedly and hence representing a delicate combination of local colour and political integration, is a touching, chaste—and, in a word, inoffensive—substitute for the proletariat. If it were once named and acknowledged, the existence of an Algerian proletariat would call forth projects of reform or even of revolution; at any rate, some empirical improvement of its real status would at least be called for. But with women there is no danger of this—you can stay in the realm of morality; nobly promote an *evolution*; shift back to a focus on the unhurried pace of civilizational progress. Above all, the diversionary operation has to do with the presentation of the very cause of the Algerian problem—to act, in Muslim lands, as though you are liberating women is surreptitiously to transform a colonial responsibility into an Islamic one; it is to suggest that women here are backward because they are subject to a religion that is widely known to subjugate them. The plan, then, is to embark the whole of colonialism on the rotten vessel of religious obscurantism and implicitly put the blame on a retrograde dogma without giving up on the alibi of 'a civilization different from our own'—a civilization whose substantive picturesqueness (the native in a *gandoura*—a long flowing gown—in front of an oil well; the black man in a loincloth harvesting 'the wealth of the tropics') is a necessary element of the ecumenism of 'greater France'. Islam provides both a convenient theme for emulation and a distracting decor—the women are integrated without being unveiled.

Les Lettres nouvelles (1 April 1959)

The Choice of a Career

**Oeuvres
complètes,**
Volume 1,
pp. 967–70

This further 'Mythologies' piece appeared in
Les Lettres nouvelles of 8 April 1959. Its subject matter is largely self-explanatory, though
it should perhaps be noted that the reference in the last paragraph to *l'Ordre moral*,
a term taken from a speech by French president Patrice de MacMahon, refers to the
French governments of the 1870s which, in
the wake of defeat by Prussia, were dominated by Royalist personnel and deeply con-
servative social and religious values.

Berthe Bernage, the daughter of a
noted Hellenist, was known mainly as the
author of the *Brigitte* series of novels,
begun in 1925. She was very active in con-
servative Catholic organizations.

Our women's magazines always have a Moral Guidance department. Since Young Ladies are reckoned the most pliant of Objects and, at the same time, the most fragile of Souls, we both dress and indoctrinate them in one fell swoop. Clothes and principles are proffered at one and the same time: proper behaviour on one page, a spring wardrobe on the other. By a happy division of labour, the young lady's outfit helps her to attract a man and the moral law helps her to hold on to him.

Moral Guidance is, therefore, an essentially defensive section of the magazine. No doubt a number of magazines of the emancipated type (such as *Elle*) are able to combine a guarded and an expansive stance, since to be positive about Woman is both to liberate her and to restrict her to her essence as Woman. But where others are concerned—and these are the very great majority of publications read by Frenchwomen—Moral Guidance is quite overtly an immobilizing technique. The point is to return woman to her *proper calling* which lies in the home.

And yet we're in the modern world and women increasingly have jobs. So the moral adviser adapts—she is helping, she says, to choose that job. In keeping with the tried and tested tactics of the great ideological institutions, the fact is apparently accepted in a spirit of liberalism but it is undermined with morality. A little progress on the one hand and a lot of regression on the other—a wide range of possibilities are presented, but, ultimately, what remains is immobility. 'Loosen up on morality, but cleave to the dogma,' said Gide's Jesuit.[1] This is how Berthe Bernage, the adviser in *L'Écho de la mode* goes about things (she has four million readers, according to a recent survey): the apparent morality is that Young Ladies may certainly work, provided that they choose a suitable occupation; the real dogma is that no occupation could actually suit them, since their natural status is to be parasitic on a man. And so they are liberally offered a choice among all the things they will ultimately be denied.

The first part of this conjuring trick consists in imagining Woman's work in its most unreal forms, in conceiving mirages of careers, after which it will be

1 In his diary entry for Christmas day 1905, Gide writes: '"Cleave to the dogma; loosen up rather on morality." This is the remark of an influential Jesuit, brought to me by Arthur Fontaine.' See Justin O'Brien (ed.), *The Journals of André Gide, Volume I: 1889–1913* (London: Secker & Warburg, 1947), p. 165. [Trans.]

easy to recommend that women lower their sights, in pretending to take dreams seriously, so as to expose their vanity afterwards. 'You want to be a star, a writer, a model? Think hard about that.' The occupation is immediately assigned to the realm of dreams: the sacred character of the star; the creative power of the artist; the perfection of the human body—in short, all those things which are seen, in our society, as magically at variance with work, since the origin of the particular function is regarded as lying in a quasi-divine gift. No doubt our Adviser imagines this gift in its lowest form as consisting in 'physical endowment' or 'the way one is': the actress' gift lies in her memory and a voice; the model is the girl who is *naturally* good-looking; women novelists and poets are those who were good at French, those who, when they were schoolgirls, could dash off a 'what I did in my holidays', a 'portrait of my grandmother' or comment on a moral proverb, exactly as Berthe Bernage does in her novel *Tout ce qui brille n'est pas de l'or* [All That Glisters Is Not Gold]. The gift is something natural that has to be *developed*. But far from study being described here as an acquisition of knowledge—or even, at the very least, as an experience—it is immediately given a moral content: work is only ever cited as a thing of virtue; it is spoken of only in terms of the courage, patience, endurance and self-control involved and of all that makes labour a form of self-denial, a test of *character* (it would seem that this moralization of labour is a pernicious myth, since we also find it under communist regimes).

Once naturalized and moralized (these are the same thing in our society), the working of talent (the way we speak of 'working' dough) logically encounters obstacles of either a natural or moral kind, which makes it possible to avoid any objective thinking about the real conditions for advancement. For our Adviser, becoming a star, a novelist or a cover girl is in no way a question of milieu, geography or background. It is difficult because you need people to 'pull strings for you'—put more euphemistically, you require 'support' (an image of a naturally immobile society emerges here, with some form of 'grace' as the only way of breaking down boundaries)—or because it is tiring (the model has her slimming programmes, the actress a more noble exhaustion from having to *get into* her role every night). But, above all, the prohibition the Adviser slaps on these prestigious careers is a moral one—one's virtue is at risk, because in them one has to mix with 'all kinds of disreputable people'.

The 'fine careers' for a woman remain: pharmacist, lab assistant, teacher or nurse. Given that these occupations may be a bit more real to the girls who read *L'Écho de la mode*, the obstacles are described in more realistic terms. The problem is the length of study required, and its cost. In short, we have descended from the Olympus of Nature and Giftedness to deal, albeit allusively, with budgetary questions, though we shall not linger long over such trivial considerations. As an inveterate moralist, Berthe Bernage cannot name a profession without bringing out the sublime element that represents both its value and its difficulty. In this case it is the vocation to 'serve'—you cannot be a pharmacist without altruism. In the daily labour of the lab assistant or the nurse, Bernage sees no other hint of alienation. Nothing about these jobs—the hours, the monotony of the work or the low wages—imposes any sort of burden, except the grandeur of the task: Do you have the necessary *vocation*?

Among these vain aspirations, then, these mirages and impossibilities, Woman seems to find no solution to her quest. But if, on this endlessly retreating occupational horizon, one career shines out as the ultimate in women's work—and our Adviser makes no bones about recommending it to her readers—it is that of domestic worker or, in other words, housemaid. This is a profession, we are told, that has changed a great deal, meaning by that, no doubt, that the domestic servant is no longer treated as an animal or an item of furniture. And what are the advantages of this career? That it strikes a happy balance, in a well-known trade-off, between the temporal (no worries about food or accommodation) and the spiritual (devotion to a Family). For, here again, the key thing is that Woman should not, at any age, throw off her dependence; that, as an incomplete individual, complementary by her very essence, like a migratory parasite—never alone, never responsible, but always *fed*—she should transplant herself from one family to another, constantly confined within a home—her parents' home as an adolescent, her husband's as a woman, and lastly, her masters' home when she is an old maid.

This parasitism is exclusive. There are, no doubt, married women who work. Berthe Bernage doesn't condemn that formula out of hand, but she judges the problem to be a *complex* one. And the complexity in question consists in eliminating little by little the fallacious advantages of two wages, in gently ushering the Woman back into a *normal* activity of life in the home: Does she not have to see to the (Christian) upbringing of the children? Thus, as in the finest days of the *Ordre moral*, Woman's Salvation lies only in landing a husband and looking after a 'home' where she will be able to live more cheaply (particularly as regards clothing). With the bubble of illusions pricked and the image of servitude enhanced with large doses of Morality, it is always the most archaic forms of our society that are to be immobilized. 'Stay where you are' is the principle of this strange form of career advice. You might think it improbable, insignificant and terribly dated, if you were not actually aware that it was the advice being handed out to four million Frenchwomen of today.

Les Lettres nouvelles (8 April 1959)

On a Use of the Verb 'To Be'

As mentioned earlier (see 'Home Knitting'), the 'Algerian War' of 1954–62 dominated French politics for much of the 1950s and 60s. It was, of course, in part a civil war within Algeria, fought between forces representing the majority of the indigenous population and the white settlers—together with a sizeable minority of Algerians—who supported l'Algérie française (i.e. continued colonial rule).

Oeuvres complètes, Volume 1, pp. 971–3

This article from Barthes's 'Mythologies' column in *Les Lettres nouvelles* of 15 April 1959 plays on the contradictions of French colonial ideology in North Africa. In retrospect, the slogan 'L'Algérie est française et le restera' (Algeria is French and will remain so) is remembered as the motto of the OAS (Organisation de l'armée secrète or Secret Army Organization), founded in January 1961 by French extreme-right paramilitaries meeting in Madrid, who hoped to reverse the French decision to withdraw from Algeria by a campaign of terrorist bombings and assassination.

Georges Bidault, mentioned in the second paragraph, was a French Christian-Democratic politician who later split from the main body of the French Right over De Gaulle's decision to withdraw from Algeria. At the time of this article, he had just left the Mouvement Républicain Populaire and was the leader of a new, but short-lived, Christian Democratic Party. As a result of his activities on behalf of L'Algérie française, he would subsequently be for a time *persona non grata* in France. When the OAS leaders were amnestied after the May 1968 'events', Bidault was included and he returned to France, though he always denied any active involvement with that terrorist organization.

'Algeria is French'

In ultra-conservative grammar, the verb 'to be' has a totalitarian function. Not only does it order the world but it also serves to express and then to *impose*, in roughly the same way that the substantive verb (*the horse is running*) first signified the whole of Aristotelian metaphysics, then, by a well-known twist, ultimately established that metaphysics as a natural Necessity (in the Middle Ages). But, further to this, it can tactically serve any purpose and is endowed with the most contradictory meanings. Expeditious, discreet and innocent, it is able, with a stroke of its magic wand, to transform judgement into fact, future wish into ancient reality and mere assertion into universal Nature. As weapon, instrument or veil, depending on the needs of the cause, it is the jack-of-all-trades of ultra-conservative rhetoric.

Its basic function is clearly to express essence. Kant may have distinguished between analytic and synthetic judgements, depending on whether or not the attribute was intrinsically related to the substance, but ultra-conservative syntax scorns any such distinction. Rudimentary and virile, it invariably subjects the whole world—in this case, Algeria—to a judgement of essence: Algeria is French in the same way as a rose is rose-coloured, porcelain fine and milk white. When all is said and done, this pleasing quality of our Algeria is a recent one; moreover, it is an entity that owes its origin to coarse considerations of possession (Georges Bidault has just stated that 'Algeria makes good business sense'). And yet, since this essence needs underwriting by something, then, as in the oldest of ideologies, it is underwritten by the Past. History here is a prior state of movement; it is conjugated exclusively in the past tense. The world did once move, but is no longer moving; what was once *done* has magically become a still, sacred state of *being*. Movement brings Profit, then Profit becomes immobilized. It becomes Right—it is my present that arrests history. This is how the 'ultra' grammar goes. It changes the functions of the verb depending upon the tense—though factual in the past tense, in the present it suddenly becomes essential. In short, what we call *the nature of things* is a curious nature—bountifully historical when explanation is being called for, it suddenly becomes *natural* when the moment of enjoyment and preservation has arrived. The French conquest was history, but the Algerian rebellion is merely an accident and perhaps even a fantasy.

This peculiar twist applied to the tense of the verb isn't innocent. The Fact being always past, and the present always being a state of Being, then if, by some truly scandalous turn of events, a present Fact dares to disturb that state of Being, it will be sufficient merely to deny it in name for it to be obliterated. Every essence has this convenient property—since it can be established by naming, it can also be destroyed by naming. This is how the facts are settled by mere denial: 'the Algerian war is virtually over', 'Algeria is just a French province, like Brittany or Picardy', etc. But in the denial itself, a shameless carving-up of reality rehabilitates the Fact each time Being feels the need to defend itself: 'There is no Algerian war', and yet there are traitors who have to be punished according to the laws of war; *Algérie française* speaks of 'ten million French people' in Algeria but at the very same time *Carrefour* magazine is indignant that 'a Muslim (Ali Khodja) who holds a representative function on behalf of the French authority, goes so far as to state . . .', etc. Doubtless there are ten million French people in Algeria, minus M. Ali Khodja who is suddenly relegated, despite the *nature of things*, into a Muslim state entirely distinct from the French authority that has been willing, conditionally, to lend it existence. A Muslim 'goes so far as to'... what a fine conception of integration! And so, like a crazed, vicious insect, we flit endlessly from an Algeria that is loftily French *in essence* to an Algeria that is *actually* torn apart, either by a rebellion that is denied at the very moment when the number of those killed or won over is being proudly reported or by the existence of masses that are neither one thing nor the other—French when they are silent and Muslim when they dare to speak.

For herein lies the drama of this 'ultra' grammar—the factor that exasperates it: the resistance of the facts. The French essence of Algeria is putative, but France's Algerian cancer is actual. On the one side are facts denied in the name of an essence, itself defined by two fantasies: a Past, and a Wish. On the other side are those same bare, stubborn, real facts against which no word can prevail magically. The rebellion *is*—and *has been* for four years—and this is a whole other sense of the verb 'to be'. Doubtless with regard to the French essence of Algeria, the secession can be defined as a barely nameable accident; it is merely a matter of assigning 'malicious' causes to it, like the telltale child who says, 'It wasn't me, it was him', blame being cast, on the one hand, on the communists, the liberals, the defeatist press and everything that isn't 'France' (since France is understood not as a nation but as a monopoly) and, on the other, on foreigners—the Russians and the Americans. But this too is wasted effort—playing down the causes doesn't alter the reality of the facts. You can always equate Algeria with the Cantal, but that district of the Auvergne hasn't risen in revolt, at least not as far as I'm aware. And if M. Ali Khodja's counterpart in the Berry region happens to pronounce on government policy, as occurs almost every Sunday in France, no one will be up in arms that a man from the Berry 'has gone so far as to say', etc. Not even the whole of 'ultra' grammar can prevail against the reality of an interminable war or of a social divide which, for its part, is the very nature of those things you did in the course of that Past from which you derive both your essence and your condemnations.

Here is what there is in 'ultra' rhetoric's verb *to be*: a frantic collusion between the indicative and the optative; the unwarranted transformation of wish into fact, of future into past, over the top of a resistant present. 'Algeria is French' has no other meaning than that it should be—by an audacious antiphrasis, *remain* is here synonymous with *become*. And even then, the second term of this equation—'French'—remains carefully selective: M. Ali Khodja is integrated into that only up to the point where he speaks; and France is the whole of France 'without distinction of race or religion' (General Allard), minus, of course, those Muslims who 'go so far as to . . .' and the 50 per cent or 60 per cent of the French (I'm not sure of the exact figure any more) who, according to a recent survey, are in favour of negotiations.[1] Ultra-conservative grammar is crowned with a metonym—in it the part is constantly being taken for the whole.

Les Lettres nouvelles (15 April 1959)

1 Negotiations between the French government and the FLN did eventually take place at Évian-les-Bains and the ensuing 'Évian Accords' ended the Algerian War with a formal ceasefire that began on 19 March 1962. In a referendum held on 8 April, more than 90 per cent of the French electorate supported the Accords. [Trans.]

On the
De Gaulle Regime

Oeuvres complètes, Volume 1, pp. 984–6

On 13 May 1958, a group of army officers mounted a *coup d'état* in Algiers, creating a *Comité de salut public* under General Massu to replace the legitimate French authorities. On 26 May, these same forces took control of Ajaccio in Corsica. In the ensuing crisis, plans were afoot for rebel army units to descend on the capital and overthrow the French government. The crisis was resolved by the return to power of General De Gaulle under a new constitution, that of the Fifth Republic, which is still in force today.

A number of French intellectuals mobilized against these events, denouncing them as 'fascistic', and the questionnaire from the 18 June 1959 issue of the magazine *14 Juillet* edited by Dionys Mascolo, to which we see Barthes responding here, was one such initiative. It was sent to 99 French intellectuals on 10 April 1959, including Jean Grosjean, René Char and Marguerite Duras. This particular document was a precursor to the famous 'Manifesto of the 121' or 'Declaration of the right to insubordination in the Algerian War', published largely on the initiative of Mascolo and Maurice Blanchot on

6 September 1960 in the magazine *Vérité-Liberté*. Among other things, it denounced the use of torture in the Algerian War and recognized that conflict as a legitimate war of independence. That was a document which Barthes famously did not sign, partly perhaps for reasons he outlines in the text below.

It should be noted that Barthes, along with the other members of the editorial board of *Arguments*, signed up to a different protest document drafted by Claude Lefort, Jean Duvignaud and Edgar Morin, entitled 'Appel à l'opinion' [Appeal to Public Opinion] published one month after the Manifesto and supported by such figures as Maurice Merleau-Ponty, Jacques Le Goff, Jacques Prévert and Paul Ricoeur.

The Monseigneur Théas referred to here was Pierre-Marie Théas, now remembered chiefly for his work in rescuing Jews during the Nazi occupation. At the time of the article, he was bishop of Tarbes and Lourdes.

1. *What happened on 13 May 1958 and what has happened since represents a set of events whose importance seems to us to have been generally underestimated. Do you believe that these are events that fall entirely within the ambit of politics? Are we not rather seeing a more serious change of direction, representing—particularly*

for thought, overtly or as yet still covertly—something like a change of horizon?

2. *If you agree with this judgement, do you not find it surprising that writers have been almost unanimously passive in the face of these events which run against the most longstanding intellectual tradition of this country? What explanation do you have for such a prolonged failure to engage?*

3. *If it is true that thought asserts itself as the contesting of what is—and in particular the contesting of Power—then doesn't the deep meaning of the democratic principle lie in the movement—a fundamental mode of the pursuit of truth—that sets thought against power and human demands against the state of things?*

4. *On that basis, isn't the government that arises out of 13 May already outside democracy, not because it might be said openly to do battle against thought, but because, basing itself on a peculiar form of sovereignty, bringing into play the exceptional destiny of a man, the potency of a providential name and the religious character of his prestige, it presents itself as a government which, by its origin and essence, lies beyond all intellectual challenge?*

5. *Does a movement of intellectual resistance to such a regime seem desirable to you? Is it possible? If so, in what form?*

Maurice Blanchot, André Breton,
Dionys Mascolo, Jean Schuster

*

What has been disorientating about General de Gaulle's accession to the presidency is the fact that it represents not so much a political as an ideological change—the liberal structures remain very largely in place, but Power has officially become sacred and been bestowed by the community on a Being of a different essence, one designated by God (the comparison of the General with Jeanne d'Arc), inspired by the Holy Spirit (the remarks of Monseigneur Théas), endowed with the power and the right to foretell the future ('I say that . . .') and ultimately a god himself, an arbitrating god, a spectator god (hence the emptiness of Gaullist policy which is an essential emptiness). As you suggest, the political interpretation of what has happened (the role of the army, the action of national capitalism, the weakness of the Left) seems to be subsumed, as it were, in a mythic interpretation—there is a general surrendering of sons to a father figure, a movement that characterizes many other current myths of the French people (the promotion of the Clear-sighted One in the press, advertising and the cinema): paternalism—not fascism, which is the (sexual) myth of the Strong Man, not the One who Knows—seems to be imposing itself as the ideology best suited to the general advancement of the middle classes.

As you so forcefully put it, it is surprising on the face of it that French intellectuals have not reacted in more essential terms to this sacralization of power, since the sacred is their true enemy—to strive perpetually against essences that are perpetually being reborn is the *raison d'être* of intellectual work. But, first, it may be that we are mistaken about ourselves; that we are, all in all, quite indifferent to the image of the Father and that we have a much more passionate relationship to the Strong Man image, whether policeman or torturer, and that we are consequently almost disappointed that Gaullism isn't fascism. Once the fascist danger of May 1958 was past, we no longer felt passionately concerned. And then, most importantly, as an ideological rather than a political regression, the advent of Gaullism found us badly unprepared. For years the cancer of political activism has stifled the intellectual's perception of the ideological. Our familiar weapons were para-political ones drawn from the revolutionary arsenal (manifestos, signatures, small groups and little magazines, etc.). Intellectual protest, which has indeed been directed more against the Stalinist regime than liberal ones, was based on a political morality or, in other words, on a range of gestures which I still see some trace of, I think, in your survey itself, containing as it does, alongside the literal meaning of the questions, an implied threat designed to divide off morally those writers who reply from those who do not.

If the meaning of Gaullism is really located at the level of ideology, we need to rediscover ideological weapons.

1. We must gradually adjust the very object of intellectual contention, directing protest less against the abuses of government and more against its alibis, its reasoning and the implicit organization of its values at all levels.

2. We should give additional substance, as it were, to the technique of intellectual combat. We should collectively assemble material on the new ideology, maintain a permanent dossier on it and perhaps open up a kind of Mythology Information Office, substituting content analyses of whatever form for ethical protestations.

3. Lastly, and most importantly, we should perhaps face up clearly to reforming the (unwritten) 'articles of association' of the French intelligentsia. We should examine the conditions in which oppositional journals could gradually merge. We should attempt to reduce intellectual factionalism or at least analyse it. In short, wherever possible, we should substitute action for gesture, and intellectual action for political action.

14 Juillet (18 June 1959)

On Left–Wing
Criticism

Oeuvres complètes, Volume 1, pp. 1083–6

This article is a response to a survey conducted by the film magazine *Positif*, a publication founded in Lyon in 1952 and generally aligned with the (non-Communist) Left. Among the other respondents were Bernard Dort, Barthes's colleague on the editorial board of *Théâtre populaire*, and the prominent film critics Philippe Esnault, Raymond Borde, Marcel Martin, Louis Seguin, Louis Marcorelles and Albert Cervoni.

The film *Come Back, Africa*, to which Barthes refers towards the end of the article, was produced and directed in 1959 by the American cineaste Lionel Ragosin. Shot in Johannesburg, Sophiatown and black areas forbidden to 'whites' under apartheid law, its plot and dialogue were largely improvised by South African 'street people' playing roles developed from their own experiences. *Come Back, Africa* was premiered at the Venice Film Festival in 1960.

The notes to the article are Barthes's own.

It is very difficult to achieve clarity around the question of left-wing criticism, which relates to the very structure of our society, to its illusions and contradictions. Particularly as we find ourselves caught immediately in a vicious circle. If we are asking what Left criticism *is*, we have to say that what is written about films in the left-wing newspapers (and what other criterion is there?) doesn't differ greatly from what is said about them elsewhere. And if the question is what left-wing criticism *should be*, then how can we set objectives for it without some preliminary idea of the Left? To force myself to speak more clearly about the subject, I would like to take your main general question and replace it with four specific ones, which I detail below.[1]

1 I do not examine how film criticism differs from the criticism of the other arts. The thoughts that follow apply to cinema and theatre, though they are somewhat less relevant to literature and much less to painting and music. Why? Because in these cases there are a great many *mediations*.

1. Does a Political Option Necessarily Entail an Ideological One?

Who can answer this question, except by following what that political option itself dictates? To say that human beings are totalities and their choices commit them in their entirety is already to commit oneself to a position. But to argue for 'freedom' of choices (that is to say, for their independence) is also to take up a position. There is no innocent answer to this question.

What happens in practice? How do the critics deal today with this connectedness of the political and the ideological? In an increasingly offhand way. We know that Marxism in France is wildly eclectic in its practice (as can be seen from *Les Lettres françaises*). Where the rest are concerned, leaving aside a number of journals with very low readerships, left-wing criticism is 'liberal'—it is not at all minded to require a link between its voting options or its political reading and what it thinks about the works of art it sees (or produces). Any intrusion of the political into the cultural seems to those critics a prelude to terror—it is, as they see it, Zdhanovism.

We have perhaps to go further: the culture of the left-wing reader is, broadly speaking—except on a number of sensitive points (such as racism)—a petty-bourgeois culture, which means that it is, to all intents and purposes, *depoliticized*. It is very significant that *France-Observateur* has never been able to politicize its cultural section, particularly where theatre and cinema are concerned. The left-wing public is apparently not calling in any sense for the development of a socialist culture—even at the cost of errors or excesses: it is likely they would find the idea unbearable.

2. What Ideological Criteria Can the Left Have?

Since the Left includes both revolutionaries and liberals, the demand for freedom always remains an ambiguous theme and not one on which we can hope to find Left unity—at least not without some deception. No doubt that unity is only to be apprehended in the deepest zones of consciousness, in a very general theme. I believe that for the Left—of whatever variety—this theme is that the human being is not a fixed entity. Man is a restless creature; he is never his own prisoner. Humanity has no essence, but only a history. Therefore every work of art that fixes the human being, that confines him in an essence of love or misfortune, that implicitly draws tragic conclusions— albeit in a cheerful or offhand way—that leads to our saying 'man is made that way' is a work of art that ought to prompt a left-wing critique (with all the nuances one might imagine). That theme is always buried in the work, especially in the cinema (13 billion viewers per year), which can never intellectualize a position. But it is precisely because decipherment is required that there is a basis for criticism. The explanatory tasks are so enormous that Left criticism has no need to concern itself with being normative: when faced with a film, let that criticism simply tell us the reasons the film gives us to live, to act, to suffer, to fight; or the reasons to do nothing and the alibis it provides; and whether the model of the human being it sketches owes his misfortune to himself, to other human beings—or to human *nature*. We shall not ask any other statement of it.

3. Is There a Left-Wing Aesthetic?

How could form itself not also be politically 'committed' or, to put it more accurately, responsible? But here again we run up against the damage done by Zdhanovism. Because a particular form of realism was imposed as the expression of a particular politics, and because that realism has generally been recognized as having no aesthetic value, the conclusion has been reached that all politically oriented art is inevitably an impoverished art. Going to the opposite extreme, the gates have been opened wide to un-realism, as though, through a sort of special privilege granted to the artist, 'form' somehow hovered in the sublime heavens of the Universal.

Yet there is someone who has taught us to think about the political commitment of form—namely, [Bertolt] Brecht. This doesn't mean that we should, from the outset, apply Brechtianism to the cinema: for specific situations, new invention is always required.

But at least we know now that audacity—including theoretical audacity—pays dividends. Let us dare to ask *everything* of a work of art: not just ideas and morality but also language—the placing of a reflector may signify a man. And, conversely, works produced in a wonderful language that are profoundly political may, for want of rigour, deliver an uncertain, insufficiently subtle argument. I am thinking here of what might have been a perfect left-wing film, *Come Back, Africa*.

4. Isn't the Politicization of Criticism Dangerous?

Once again, Zdhanovism casts a very dark shadow. Because the politicization of art occurred in a regime that imposed it by the harshest coercion, we have rejected it wholesale, to such a degree that the rejection of terror turns, at times, into a counter-terror. Is it so difficult to be discriminating in these matters? It is one thing—and a detestable one—to infringe the temporal freedom of creation, but it is quite another to ask the artist to be responsible for his work. Much more than this, by a paradox that is merely a ruse of history, it is precisely because we are living in a (still) liberal democracy, in which artists are (relatively) free, that their political responsibility should be at its fullest. It is in a bourgeois regime that we have to call for a politicized criticism, and there is no sophistry in this. Temporal freedom and political responsibility—this, it seems to me, should be the chief watchword of a socialist culture.[2]

Positif (November 1960)

2 I applaud, for example, the fact that Ionesco is performed in Yugoslavia. To the same degree I deplore the fact that there is no political criticism of his plays there.

ROLAND BARTHES

A Case of
Cultural Criticism

On the initiative of Georges Friedmann, the November 1969 issue of the École pratique's journal *Communications* (NO. 14) was devoted to the subject of cultural policy. The editorial foreword first referenced the creation of the French Ministry of Cultural Affairs and the state-run *maisons de la culture*, though the uprising of May 1968 was also alluded to, with particular emphasis on the perception of the May events as a 'cultural revolution'. This article by Barthes is the last in a section entitled 'Situation et contestation de l'action culturelle'. Whereas the others largely examine the question of state cultural policy—albeit, in Violette Morin's case, through the person of De Gaulle's minister of culture André Malraux—Barthes's contribution is a brief essay on the hippy phenomenon in a North African town.

Oeuvres complètes, Volume 3, pp. 104–7

The town where these lines are being written is a small gathering place for hippies—mainly British, American and Dutch ones. They spend all day occupying a very lively square in the old town, mingled in among (but not mixing with) the local population, who, whether out of natural tolerance, amusement, habit or interest, accept them, brush along with them and let them get on with their lives, not understanding them but showing no surprise either. There isn't the density or variety of the great gatherings in San Francisco or New York, but since 'the hippy phenomenon' is outside its normal context here, which is that of a rich, moralizing civilization, its ordinary meaning breaks down. Transplanted into a rather poor country and out of his normal environment—not through any geographical exoticism but through economic and social exoticism (which is infinitely more divisive)—the hippy becomes something contradictory (and not merely contrary). And his contradictoriness is of interest because, at the level of protest, it brings into question the very relationship between the political and the cultural.

This contradictoriness consists in the fact that the hippy, as an oppositional figure, stands opposed to the main values underpinning the Western (bourgeois, neo-bourgeois or petty-bourgeois) way of life. He knows that way of life is a way of consumption, and it is the consumption of goods he is out to undermine. Where food is concerned, the hippies throw off all constraints of times and menus (they eat little, anytime and anywhere) or of individual dining (when we eat in a group, we do so only in an accumulation of individual servings, as is symbolized now by the use of those cloth or straw place mats which, in the name of elegance, mark out the nutritive space of each diner. By contrast, hippies—at Berkeley, for example—use a collective pot and eat communally). There is the same collectivism about living arrangements—one room for several people. And to this we can add nomadism, as flagged up by the bag or pouch the hippies have dangling down around their long legs. As we know, their clothing (their costume, we should call it) is the hippies' specific sign, their major choice. As regards the Western norm, they subvert it in two—at times combined—directions: either by being wildly fantastical, by exceeding the limits of convention in such a way as to produce a clear mark of transgression (brocade trousers; draped jackets; long white nightshirts; bare feet); or by an intrusive borrowing from local costume—*djellabas*, *boubous*, Hindu tunics—but cut across by some aberrant detail, such as necklaces or multicoloured chokers. Cleanliness (hygiene), the leading American value (at least in mythic terms), is spectacularly flouted with dirt about the body, in the hair or on the clothes, material dragging along the ground, dust-covered feet, fairhaired toddlers playing in the gutter (though an undefinable distinction remains between authentic dirt, the dirt of very old poverty, which *deforms* the body and the hand, and this borrowed, holiday dirt spread over things like dust, not ingrained in them). Lastly, with the boys' long hair and jewellery (necklaces, multiple rings, earrings), the sexes are scrambled, being not so much inverted as obliterated: what is being sought, through a switching between ordinarily distinctive features, is the neutral—a challenge to the 'natural' antagonism between the sexes.

We are not talking here about the 'inward' countervalues that are part of the hippy movement: the use of drugs, 'dropping out' and the elimination of aggression. At the simple phenomenal level, it is quite clear that hippy *mores* are intended as a radicalization of a *reaction*. Clothing, living arrangements, food, hygiene and sexuality are turned around here into *reactive* forces. This word should be understood in a Nietzschean sense. Paradoxical as it may seem, the hippy (at least if he put more intelligence into his adventure and exploration) could be one of the prefigurings of the Overman— that precursor which Nietzsche saw in the last nihilist, the one who attempts to generalize the reactive value and push it to the point where it cannot be recuperated by any sort of positive force. We know that Nietzsche pointed to two historical incarnations of this nihilism: Christ and the Buddhist. And these are, in fact, the two hippy dreams. The hippy phenomenon looks towards India (which is becoming the Mecca of the movement) and many young hippies (too many for it to be insignificant) are clearly intent on adopting a Christ-like appearance. We are talking about symbols here, not beliefs (the present writer saw a local crowd surround and threaten, with thoroughly oriental vehemence, a long-haired, pale-faced young Christ who was accused of stealing a radio—the facts of the situation are not at all clear, but they fitted into the local *code* of theft—and this produced an authentically evangelical scene, a pious picture fit to adorn a pastor's hallway). This is one of the directions the hippy phenomenon is going in and one of its meanings.

Yet this meaning (and this is the contradiction we spoke about at the beginning) is hijacked by the context in which reality compels it to develop. In the US, the hippy's cultural protest is effective (straightforward, we might say) because it strikes *precisely* (at the sensitive points) against the good consciences of the well-to-do, of those who claim ownership of morality and hygiene. In that case, hippyism represents a justified stage (even if a somewhat rudimentary one) in cultural criticism, since it exactly points up the hollowness of the American way of life. But outside its original context, hippy protest encounters a much more formidable adversary than American conformism, even when supported by campus police. That adversary is poverty (where economics speaks euphemistically of *developing countries*, the local culture and art of living clearly bespeak poverty). That poverty *transforms* the hippy option into a caricature of economic alienation, and this—flippantly flaunted—caricature ends up, as a result, replete with positive irresponsibility. For most of the characteristics developed by the hippies in opposition to their civilization of origin (which is an affluent one) are the very characteristics distinctive of poverty, not in this case as signs, but, much more seriously, as physical effects or markers: the lack of proper meals, collective living, going barefoot, dirtiness and raggedness are not in this case forces in the symbolic struggle against the excess of material goods, but real conditions that have to be combatted. Symbols (which the hippy consumes frantically) are no longer now reactive meanings, polemical forces or the weapons of a criticism taken from an affluent civilization that neutralizes its excessive food consumption by constantly speaking of it and works to convert its signifiers into markers of abundant nature; having switched from the side of positivity, they cease in any sense to belong to a *game*, a higher form of symbolic activity, and become a *disguise*, a lower form of cultural narcissism. The context, as is the rule with language, overturns the meaning—and the context here is economics.

This is the impasse in which a cultural criticism cut off from its political argument finds itself. But is there another way? Can we conceive of a political critique of culture—an active, and not merely analytical, critique—that would find a place for itself way beyond the ideological conditioning of mass communications at those very—subtle, diffuse—sites of consumer conditioning—the precise points where the hippies bring their (incomplete) perceptiveness to bear? Can we imagine an art of living that would be, if not revolutionary, then at least *disengaged*? No one since [Charles] Fourier has produced such an image; no figure can be substituted for the political activist and the hippy in such a way as to combine them. The activist goes on living like a petty-bourgeois; the hippy lives like a *reverse*-bourgeois. Between the two there is nothing—the political and cultural critiques are unable to come together.

Communications (November 1969)

So,
How Was China?

*Oeuvres
complètes,*
Volume 4,
pp. 516–20

Between 11 April and 4 May 1974, at the
height of the Cultural Revolution, a delegation from *Tel Quel* travelled to China. The
trip had been suggested by the Italian left-
wing journalist Maria-Antonietta Macciocchi,
author of the controversial work *Dalla Cina*
[*On China*] (Milan: Feltrinelli, 1971), a book
that had been banned from the bookstalls of
the French Communist Party's annual festival
when it appeared in translation [*De la Chine*
(Paris: Seuil, 1971)] and that eventually led to
her exclusion from the Italian party. It is said
that Macciocchi was keen to repay the *Tel
Quel* group for their support at the time of
the controversy, though they themselves
were split over the new pro-Chinese line:
Jean Thibaudeau and Jean Ricardou were
pushed into resignation over it, while Jacques
Derrida and Jean-Joseph Goux distanced
themselves considerably.

The arrangements for the journey were
largely made by Philippe Sollers, who chose
Julia Kristeva, Marcelin Pleynet, François
Wahl, Jacques Lacan and Barthes to accom-
pany him. Lacan withdrew at the last moment
for reasons that are not entirely clear.

Much ink has been spilt about Barthes's motivation for making the trip. It seems he was genuinely interested in China's ancient culture and civilization, being greatly influenced in this by the writings of the Cambridge historian of Chinese science Joseph Needham, and he spent considerable time making preparations for the visit, including some work on the language. Though he appears to have been the first person to suggest that the group purchase Mao costumes when they arrived, all accounts suggest that he very soon became disaffected with the experience and retreated into a weary indifference. Though he showed enthusiasm for certain aspects of Chinese life, such as calligraphy, the organized visits appear to have bored him and he notoriously stayed in the car the day the delegation visited the famous Ming tombs near Beijing and sat apart from the others, reading Flaubert's *Bouvard et Pécuchet*, during a train journey to Nanjing (Marcelin Pleynet, *Le Voyage en Chine*, pp. 54, 46). Reviewing the notebooks on which this present article were based when they were finally published in 2009, Sollers wrote: 'Poor Barthes! He was 59 years old and I rather forced his hand over this trip . . .' ('Le supplice chinois de Roland Barthes. Sur les *Carnets du voyage en Chine*' [Roland Barthes's Chinese Ordeal. On the *Carnets du voyage en Chine*], *Le Nouvel Observateur*, 29 January 2009). Barthes would later tell the students at his seminar that he felt distanced from the country by the fact that there seemed to be 'no role for the body' in China

(*Le lexique de l'auteur*, 8 May 1974, p. 234) and, in an interview with Bernard-Henri Lévy, he expressed clear distaste for the moralism of the regime ('A quoi sert un intellectual?', *Le Nouvel Observateur*, 10 January 1977; reprinted in *Oeuvres complètes*, VOL. 5, pp. 364–82).

All the participants produced some account of their visit when they returned, with only that of François Wahl being overtly critical (F. Wahl, 'La Chine sans utopie', *Le Monde*, 15–19 June 1974). Unsurprisingly, Sollers availed himself of the columns of *Tel Quel* to answer the criticisms ('Réponse à François Wahl', *Tel Quel* 59, Autumn 1974).

This article embodying Barthes's reactions was published by *Le Monde* on 24 May 1974. Barthes's first biographer Louis-Jean Calvet describes it as giving 'the impression that he does not want to say anything' (*Roland Barthes: A Biography*. Cambridge: Polity Press, 1994, p. 201), while Tiphaine Samoyault notes a surprising 'absence of critical spirit' (*Roland Barthes*. Paris: Seuil, 2015, p. 506).

In the calm shade of the rooms where we are received, our interlocutors (workers, teachers and peasants) are patient, assiduous (everyone takes notes; there's no sense of boredom, but a peaceable feeling of working together) and, above all, attentive—not to our identity but to our listening, as though, when confronted with some unknown intellectuals, it was still important for this vast people to be acknowledged and understood; as though what was required of foreign friends here was not to show solidarity in struggle, but assent.

You set out for China armed with a thousand pressing and, it seems, natural questions: How do things stand there with regard to sexuality, women, the family and morality? What is the state of the human sciences, linguistics or psychiatry? We shake the tree of knowledge so that the answer will fall and we'll be able to come home bearing our main form of intellectual sustenance—a secret deciphered. But nothing falls. In a sense (apart from the political answer), we come home with—*nothing*.

You then turn to questioning yourself: What if these objects, which we want at all costs to turn into questions (sex, the subject, language, science) were merely historical and geographical particularities, civilizational idioms? We want there to be impenetrable things so that we can penetrate them: by ideological atavism, we are creatures of decipherment, hermeneutic subjects; we believe our intellectual task is always to uncover a meaning. China seems reluctant to deliver up this meaning, not because it hides it but, more subversively, because (in a way that is far from Confucian) it undoes the constitution of concepts, themes and names; it doesn't divide up the targets of knowledge as we do; the semantic field is disorganized; the question asked indiscreetly of meaning is turned round into a question of meaning in general, and our knowledge turned into a phantasmagoria—the ideological objects our society constructs are silently declared *impertinent*. It is the end of hermeneutics.

So we leave behind us the turbulence of symbols and enter upon a very big, very old, very new country, where meaning [*signifiance*] is discreet to the point of rarity. At that moment, a new field opens up, the field of delicacy or, more precisely (I'll venture the word, even if I have to take it back later), of blandness.

Apart from its ancient palaces, its posters, its children's ballets and its first of May, China isn't *in colour*. The countryside (at least the countryside we saw, which isn't the countryside of the old paintings) is flat. There are no historical objects to break it up (neither church towers nor manor houses); in the distance, all that's to be seen is a couple of grey oxen, a tractor, some regular though asymmetrical fields and a group of workers dressed in blue. The rest, as far as the eye can see, is beige (tinged with pink) or pale green (wheat and rice); there are at times patches of yellow rape or that purple flower that is used, it seems, as green manure, but these are still pale. There's no change of scenery.

The green tea is bland. It is served up on all occasions and your lidded cup is regularly refreshed, but it seems only to exist to punctuate meetings, discussions and trips with a thin, gentle ritual. From time to time you take a few gulps of tea and light a cigarette and, in this way, words take on a silent, serene quality (the way the work we saw in the workshops we visited seemed silent and serene). Tea-drinking is a thing of good manners, even friendship, but there is a distant quality in it. It makes chumminess, effusiveness and the whole theatre of social relations seem excessive.

As for the body, the apparent eclipse of any concern with physical appearance (fashion or make-up), the uniformity of clothing, the prosaic nature of gesture—all these absences, multiplied across an enormous population, prompt the unprecedented—and perhaps heart-rending—impression that the body is no longer to be understood, that over there it is stubbornly set upon not signifying, on not being captured by any erotic or dramatic reading (except on stage).

Did I say blandness? Another, more accurate word suggests itself: China is *peaceful*. Isn't peace (to which Chinese onomastics refers so often) that—to us, utopian—region where the war of meanings is abolished? Over there, meaning is cancelled, exempted in all the places where we Westerners pursue it; but it remains standing—armed, articulate and on the offensive—where we are reluctant to put it: in politics.

Signifiers (the things that exceed meaning, cause it to overflow and to press on, towards desire) are rare. Here are three, however, in no particular order: first, cookery, which is, as we know, the most complex in the world; then, because there's an enormous, boundless quantity of them, children, whom one never wearies of watching avidly, so varied are their expressions (which are never affected) and always so incongruous; and, lastly, writing. This last is, no doubt, the major signifier. In the wall-mounted manuscripts (they are everywhere), the brush of the anonymous calligrapher (a worker or peasant)—who (as we noted in a writing workshop) is incredibly 'driven'—hurls the pressures of his body and the tensions of the struggle into a single act. And the calligraphy of Mao, reproduced on every scale, stamps Chinese space (a factory hall, a park, a bridge) with its great lyrical, elegant, wavy signature. This is a wonderful art that is present everywhere, and more convincing (to us) than the heroic hagiography of foreign origin.

All in all, China presents very little to be read but its political Text. That Text is everywhere and every area of activity is included in it. In all the discourses we heard, Nature (the natural, the eternal) no longer speaks (except on one curiously resistant point, the family, which seems to be spared in the criticism currently levelled against Confucius).

And yet, there again, to find Text (what we call Text today), you have to go through an enormous swathe of repetitions. Every discourse seems to advance by a series of commonplaces (*topoi* and clichés) analogous to those sub-routines that cybernetics refers to as 'building blocks'. So is there no freedom? Certainly there is.

Beneath its rhetorical crust, the Text is bubbling with life (desire, intelligence, struggle, work; all that divides, overflows, comes through).

First, everyone combines these clichés differently, not as part of an aesthetic project of originality but under the variably intense pressure of his/her political consciousness (what a difference we found, within this same code, between the wooden speech of an official of a People's Commune and the lively, precise, apposite analysis of a worker in a naval dockyard in Shanghai!). Then, like an epic narrative, the discourse always *represents* the struggle between two 'lines'. Doubtless we foreigners only ever hear the voice of the triumphant line, but that triumph is never triumphalist. It is a *warning cry*, a move by which the revolution is constantly prevented from growing flabby, glutted and set in its ways. Lastly, this apparently highly coded discourse in no way excludes inventiveness and, I would go so far as to say, a certain playfulness. Take the current campaign against Confucius and Lin Piao. It gets everywhere and takes a thousand forms. Its very name (in Chinese: *Pilin Pikong*) tinkles like a merry little bell, and the campaign divides into so many invented games—a caricature, a poem, a sketch acted by children, in which a little girl in make-up suddenly rounds on the ghost of Lin Piao between two dance routines. The political Text (and it alone) generates these minor 'happenings'.

Michelet equated the France he dreamed of with a great piece of prose, a neutral, smooth, transparent state of language and sociality. In its attenuation of faces, in its mixing of social strata (this is probably the same thing), China is eminently prosaic. This country—the site of a great historical experiment—isn't encumbered with heroism. One might say heroism 'gathers' here, as in an abscess, on the opera or ballet stage or in posters, where the Women are always the ones whose role it is (out of respect for them or malice?) to raise their political hackles. In the streets, workshops and schools and on the country roads, by contrast, a people (which in 25 years has already built up a substantial nation) moves around, works, drinks its tea or performs its solitary exercises without drama, noise or posturing—in short, without hysteria.

Le Monde (24 May 1974)

*

[When this short text was published in a slim volume by Christian Bourgois in 1975, the following afterword was added.]

October 1975:

By the few (negative) reactions it has prompted, this circumstantial text raises, as I see it, a question of principle—not what is it *permitted*, but what is it *possible,* to say or not to say? Every idiom involves some obligatory rubrics—not only does language, by its structure, prevent us from saying certain things, since there is no grammatical expression that enables us to say them, but it also forces us positively to say other things. For example, with how many words, which we for our own part would wish to treat as undifferentiated, are we forced to choose between the masculine and feminine genders because our language includes those two rubrics and those two alone? We French people are compelled to speak masculine/feminine.

Because it is the product of a combinatory of sentences, discourse is, in theory, entirely free—there is no obligatory structure of discourse, except the rhetorical. And yet, as a result of a mental constraint—of civilization or ideology—our discourse also has its obligatory rubrics. We cannot speak—and, particularly, we cannot write—without being subject to one of the following modes: assertion, denial, doubt or questioning. And yet cannot the human subject have a different desire—the desire to *suspend* his utterance, without for all that abolishing it.

On China, an immense object—and, for many, a hotly debated one—I tried to produce (this was where my truth lay) a discourse that was neither assertive, negative nor neutral. I tried to produce a commentary whose tone would be one of 'no comment'; an assent (a mode of language of the order of an ethics and perhaps of an aesthetics) and not necessarily an adherence or a rejection (modes which, for their part, are of the order of reason or faith). By gently hallucinating China as an object located outside bright colours, strong flavours and stark meanings (all these things being not unconnected with the sempiternal parading of the phallus), I wanted to bind in a single movement the infinite feminine (maternal?) quality of the object itself, that unprecedented way China had, as I saw it, of peacefully and powerfully exceeding meaning, and the right to a special discourse, the discourse of a gentle drifting or, alternatively, of a wish for silence or for 'wisdom' perhaps, that word being understood more in a Taoist than a Stoic sense ('The perfect Tao offers no difficulty, except that it avoids choosing . . . Don't oppose the world of the senses . . . The wise man does not struggle').

This negative hallucination isn't gratuitous—it seeks to respond to the way many Westerners hallucinate the People's Republic of China in a dogmatic, violently affirmative/negative or falsely liberal way. Isn't it ultimately a shabby idea of politics to think that it can only find expression in the form of a *directly* political discourse? The intellectual (or the writer) has no place. Or that place is no other than the Indirect. It is for this utopia that I tried to provide a discourse that is right or true (musically). We have to love music—including Chinese music.

Utopia

This short text was originally published in an Italian translation in the *Almanacco Bompiani* for 1974 (Milan: Bompiani, 1974). It did not appear in French until Éric Marty included it in Barthes's Complete Works. It was the Einaudi publishing house of Turin that was largely responsible for the publication of Barthes's work in Italian translation, though Bompiani did publish in book form an article on rhetoric which Barthes had originally written for *Communications*: *La retorica antica* (Paolo Fabbri trans.) (Milan: Bompiani, 1972).

Oeuvres complètes, Volume 4, pp. 531–2

Utopia is the field of desire, as opposed to Politics which is the field of need. Hence the paradoxical relations between these two discourses—they complement but do not comprehend each other. Need resents Desire's irresponsibility and triviality; Desire resents Need's strictures and its reductive power. Sometimes the Wall is penetrated and Desire manages to explode into Politics. This produces something like May '68, a rare historic moment, the moment of an *immediate utopia*—the occupied Sorbonne lived for a month in a utopian state (it was, in effect, 'nowhere').

Desire should constantly be brought back into politics. By this I mean not only that utopias are justified but also that they are necessary. We might even say it is an indication of the dullness of our age that we are currently unable to compose utopias. It is as though we are reluctant to imagine them—we are in thrall to the great political Superego. Truth to tell, it isn't that we are afraid to produce a general blueprint for a future society—such things are to be found, and to be found in the political sphere. It is the *details* of that society we will not give, and this is where utopian thinking and desire is lacking, for utopias—this is their particular nature—are *minutely detailed*. Utopian thinking imagines timetables, places, practices; it is *romanesque*—novelistic—like the fantasy, of which it is ultimately simply the political form.

Utopia is always ambivalent: it is devastating in its take on the present, endlessly stressing what is wrong in the world and, at the same time—and to the same extent—it conjures up images of happiness. It conjures them up in all their colourfulness and sparkle, in all their precision and even their absurdity. It has that rarest of things—the courage to enjoy. Sade and Fourier, the two greatest utopians I know, had that courage. Of course, no utopia has the slightest chance of being applied as a total system. The Fourierist *phalanstère* and the Sadean château are, literally speaking, impossible. But it is the elements, the inflections, the obscurer nooks and crannies of the utopian system that reappear in our world as flashes of desire, as thrilling possibilities. If we were more receptive to them, they would prevent Politics from congealing into a totalitarian, bureaucratic, moralistic system.

Almanacco Bompiani 1974
(Milan: Bompiani, 1974)

Mythology

***Oeuvres completes,* Volume 4, p. 570**

This short piece in *Le Figaro* of 8 October 1974 is Barthes's reply to the survey 'The Intellectuals in Question', conducted by Renaud Matignon on the occasion of the publication of Georges Suffert's *Les Intellectuels en chaise longue* (Paris: Plon, 1974). Matignon was one of the founders of *Tel Quel*, though he distanced himself very quickly from that magazine. This is a rare contribution by Barthes to the right-wing *Le Figaro*, though Barthes did grant Laurent Kissel of its literary supplement an interview in 1975 ('Roland Barthes met le langage en question', *Le Figaro littéraire*, 5 July 1975).

To speak of the party of the intellectuals is comical. There is indeed in our society a group or, let us say, a caste that vaguely includes writers, philosophers and teachers that might be called the intellectual caste. But let's leave chaises-longues out of it—the intellectual's situation is historically uncomfortable and dialectically ambiguous, precisely because of the contradictions of our society.

What there is in France is a temptation towards anti-intellectualism. This mythological nonsense has its origins in Romanticism, in 'thinking with the heart rather than the head' and other such balderdash. But its petty-bourgeois character is very clearly in evidence— that very attitude that not so long ago gave rise to Poujadism. It is the expression of a retrograde political stance.

The intellectual continues to be needed by all bourgeois societies, like the medicine man in the primitive tribe who takes the evil upon himself. It is his duty to dispel alienated consciousness. There are those who would like to confine him to his ghetto. The intellectual is without power, but that doesn't mean he cannot act.

Le Figaro (8 October 1974)

Letter to
Bernard–Henri Lévy

Oeuvres complètes, Volume 5, pp. 314–5

This letter was written in response to B.-H. Lévy's book *La Barbarie à visage humain* (Paris: Grasset, 1977) and published in *Les Nouvelles littéraires* of 26 May 1977. Lévy's book is generally regarded as the second major contribution, after André Glucksmann's *La Cuisinière et le mangeur d'hommes, réflexions sur l'État, le marxisme et les camps de concentration* (Paris: Seuil, 1975), to the current of thinking that became known as 'la nouvelle philosophie', which was seen by some as a genuine attempt to grapple with the problematic relationship between Marxism and totalitarianism and by others as an opportunistic power-grab within the French journalistic and media scene. Lévy's *La Barbarie* was directed partly against Marxist totalitarianism and partly against fashionable 'ideologies of desire'. With his remark on Deleuze, Barthes is careful to distance himself from the latter aspect.

I just want to pen a quick note to convey the particular way your book moves me. I have, admittedly,
had a very personal relationship with the ideas you
express—most, as you know, are too close to home
(those, roughly, relating to the crisis of historical tran-
scendence), while others are more distant (your criticism of Deleuze seems to me misguided). But what
enchanted me (the word should be taken to convey
pleasure, solidarity and fascination) is that your book
is *written*. To some important ideas—which will surely
be seen as belonging to the field of politics—you have
given the grain of an *écriture*, which is not a common
occurrence.

Though this is a book of ideas, positions and arguments, you have, in fact, taken it upon yourself to *write*
the book—that is to say, to endow it with that charac-
teristic, that excess, that act [*geste*] which detaches
what is written from mere *écrivance* and makes it part
of another kind of exchange that has constraints,
effects and stakes which we are trying today to
describe, because we wish to wrest it from the unimag-
inative conceptions of a technicistic society that flat-
tens writing into mere speech, reduces the utterance

to a message and makes enunciation a mere instrument. In short, we are trying to convey that language is a *passion* or, if you prefer a 'pathos', provided that this word (and I hope it does not shock you) is understood as having the *noble* connotations Nietzsche lent to it when he spoke, favourably, of a 'pathos of distance'.

By this I am suggesting that writing today is a militant act (a 'modern' one, let us say), and in no sense a return to a merely decorative activity. I am happy to take over, though in a different context, [Giacomo] Leopardi's saying (and here I quote from memory) that '*Bello scrivere* is a very profound and subtle philosophy . . .' It seems to me that, in depicting a certain historical pessimism (or providing arguments for it— the two are the same to me) and, particularly, in discussing the relations between power and language, you could not but produce a genuine writing [*écriture*]— and could not but do so, I would say, in the stylistic fullness of the term. This is the point where your book prompts a hypothesis that may be dangerous, but which I can venture in a letter without fear of consequences: Might there not be a kind of fit between the optimistic ideology of historical 'progress' and the instrumentalist conception of language? And conversely, might there not be the same relationship between every critical distancing of history and the subversion of intellectual language by writing? After all, the *ars scribendi*, as successor to the art of oratory, was associated historically with a displacement of political speech (a shift away from politics as pure speech). Your project is merely beginning this displacement anew, which had been lost to view since people stopped *writing* politics—that is to say, since Rousseau.

These remarks, confined to what is generally termed a formal question, will perhaps seem limited and your book is, of course, far wider in scope. But it seemed more appropriate to me to point out how this book hinges on that 'ethics of writing' that currently interests me.

Les Nouvelles littéraires (26 May 1977)

The Minorities
of the Minorities

Oeuvres complètes, Volume 5, pp. 449–50

Barthes made several contributions in his latter years to *Le Nouvel Observateur* (then by some distance the most popular left-wing magazine in France), including reviews of books, films and exhibitions, interviews on topical subjects, and even a commentary on the weeks' 'cultural programme'. This review of Haim Zafrani's book, *Études et recherches sur la vie intellectuelle juive au Maroc de la fin du XVe siecle au début du XXe siècle. Tome 2: Poésie juive en Occident musulman* [Studies and Research on Jewish Intellectual Life in Morocco from the Fifteenth to the Twentieth Centuries: Volume 2, Jewish Poetry of the Muslim West] (Paris: Éditions Geuthner), appeared on 16 January 1978.

The recent interview with Zafrani to which Barthes refers in this article was published in *Le Monde* of 30–31 October 1977.

A good work of literature is often worth a whole host of political writings. In exploring a small field apparently neglected by everyone—namely, the Jewish poetry of the Muslim West—Haim Zafrani casts doubt on some of our prejudices. Ultimately, isn't that what we should tirelessly ask scholarly books to do?

We are used to seeing literature as the natural product of a dominant civilization that is solidly established on its territory. In our eyes, literature is always more or less the ornament of political power. Haim Zafrani, by contrast, speaks to us of a minority, migratory literature, a literature beset by the constraints of isolation, exile, marginality. We are used to believing words to be the individual property of those who use them. Zafrani speaks to us of a literature free of any mark of ownership, in which verses, formulations and feelings circulate from one author to another and in which everyone has, as a result, a '*presumption of ownership*' over the entire heritage of forms.

We are used to regarding it as the natural function of poetry to interpret 'the lessons and silences of nature', as Sartre puts it—or of 'the body', as we should say today. Zafrani speaks to us of a poetry stirred more by ideas than landscape. This extends a long way beyond the concern of specialists: everything that *pluralizes* the—often very egoistical—idea we have of culture interests us; to shine a searchlight, as Zafrani does, onto a literature that isn't far removed from our own in space (Morocco isn't far) and yet is neither pagan, Christian nor Arabic, is as justified an undertaking as the pluralization of music, which some are trying to achieve today. In the eighteenth century, a battle was fought for tolerance (a poor word, as it happens) in the name of human unity; in our own day, the same battle is being fought (I mean to say, a battle that is just as necessary) but in the name of difference, inasmuch as we are determined not to diminish it.

In a recent interview, Haim Zafrani reminded us of the scale and diversity of the cultural achievements made over centuries among these two—Muslim and Jewish—communities of the Maghreb. His book shows that poetry was one of the main fields in which this Judaeo-Arabic exchange took place. For a poetry that was wholly fascinated by the Bible and the Davidic model and intimately bound up with worship, it was a difficult wrench to shift to secular forms. It was very much under the powerful influence of Arabic literature that a secular Hebrew poetry was born in Andalusian Spain. And that poetry quite naturally adopted Arabic metric schemes (a problem which Voltaire already discussed in his day).

Now, in everything that happens at the level of language—and poetry is, in a sense, the effort a language makes to represent its power to itself—something of that monumental history which political divisions so often oppress and conceal always shows through; for language is enunciation or, in other words, the place the subject attributes to himself in the world. Zafrani's work gives us an idea of—and a desire for—another history than the history of oppressions, exclusions and divisions: the history, or the structural affinity, of these peoples' languages.

Lastly, though he is speaking of an apparently distant, exotic phenomenon, Zafrani brings out something extremely topical and urgent—something that is perhaps new in political sociology. He shows how the rabbinical authorities and Talmudic scholarship always regarded poetry as a suspect genre, and also how a number of Jewish academics today exclude the poetry of the Eastern Diaspora from their study, research and teaching, thus consigning it to oblivion. Of course, this censorship is no innocent matter: it represses Sephardic poetic production, which was freer, more lyrical and more individualistic, in the name of a more communal (Ashkenazi) culture—a move that is always dangerous. For in a world in which power invariably reconstitutes itself very rapidly in those very places where a battle has been waged for its destruction, what we can still call 'freedom', 'creativity' and 'vitality' increasingly take refuge in those fragile, temporary spaces that are 'the minorities of the minorities'.

Le Nouvel Observateur (16 January 1978)

Remarks on Violence

This interview with Jacqueline Sers, which appeared in the Protestant journal *Réforme* of 2 September 1978, was prefaced on its publication by the following remarks: 'Many of the themes that preoccupy public opinion and fill the columns of the newspapers throughout the year fade from view during the holiday period. Violence is one of these. Because we frequently speak too much about violence—and speak about it badly— a programme in the [television] series Présence Protestante will be devoted to this theme. It was for that reason that Jacqueline Sers went to ask Roland Barthes—writer, analyst and teacher—to unpick the word "violence", as he has unpicked other terms with such skill and zest in his *Mythologies*. This is, then, an exclusive interview for *Réforme*, but echoes of it will be heard in the Présence Protestante programme of Sunday 3 September 1978 (10 a.m. on TF1), which will also have contributions from Jacqueline Sers, Danielle Levy-Alvarès (journalist), Prof. G. Menut, Dr Y. Roumageon and Jacques Barrot (director of a hostel for the homeless).'

Oeuvres complètes, Volume 5, pp. 549–53

JACQUELINE SERS. You told me very kindly that you'd be happy to be interviewed by *Réforme* ... Why was that?

ROLAND BARTHES. For sentimental reasons. I had a Protestant childhood. My mother was Protestant and I came to know Protestantism well during my adolescence. I can even say that it interested me, raised questions for me and I became involved in it. Then I moved away. But I've always retained a sentimental attachment— more perhaps to Protestants than to Protestantism. Perhaps on account of that goodwill one always feels towards minorities.

SERS. Above and beyond all the definitions that go with celebrity, who are you, Roland Barthes?

BARTHES. I've taken part in many types of intellectual activity, both in the theory of meaning and in literary and social criticism and so on. But if there's a good word to describe what's going on inside me—though not in my writings—it would be the word 'philosopher', though this doesn't refer here to a specific type of competence because I have no philosophical training.

What I'm doing inside is philosophizing, thinking about what's happening to me. I find joy and profit in that, and when I'm prevented from doing it, I feel a little unhappy and deprived of something important. Philosophizing perhaps belongs more to the ethical than the metaphysical order . . .

*

SERS. Could you dissect the word violence, which we see used widely today, in the same way as you've dissected other words from the French vocabulary in your *Mythologies*?

BARTHES. When you throw the word out like this, you realize it's entirely heteroclite and prompts in you a kind of panic in your reactions and responses.

It's a word that's understood differently by many very different people and it covers very different things. You may have a narrow understanding of violence, but as you come to think more about it, its meaning expands infinitely. This is a first difficulty, of an intellectual, analytical sort—all the more so as the word lends itself easily to discussion, since it's already fixed and constrained in its meaning within legal reports, documents and processes. And there are all kinds of screens placed in front of this word by mass culture itself.

The second difficulty is of an existential order. Violence affects our bodies—we therefore have reactions to it that are generally reactions of rejection or refusal. But there are perhaps human beings who are at ease with violence and even find a sort of fulfilment in it. Violence doesn't refer to something simple.

The third difficulty is that it's a word that raises problems of behaviour for states, communities and individuals. One actually feels very much at a loss here. It's a problem as old as the hills: How are we to keep down violence except by other violence?

This brings us to a kind of impasse that ends up having a religious dimension to it. That's an awful lot of difficulties and we have, in a way, to accept a sort of powerlessness in the face of this word. It's insoluble.

SERS. Why this reference to a religious dimension with regard to the word 'violence'?

BARTHES. There isn't a religion in the world—at least among the religions of the great civilizations, East and West—that hasn't taken on board the problem of violence in a general conception of a metaphysical kind, either by equating it with evil or, conversely, in some more archaic religions, with the law. The fact of a religion taking on the problem would imply the need for conversion to deal with it. If you want to deal with it in secular terms, then you need to find another key. To deal with violence, you have to choose your key.

SERS. If violence is 'insoluble', as you put it, then is there no key to it in secular terms?

BARTHES. In the religious dimension, it's equally insoluble—temporally! That it's soluble spiritually is possible—or even certain—but that's not for me to say.

But to come back to the level of intellectual analysis, we have to be aware that there are several types of violence.

There's the violence that lies in any constraint imposed by the community on the individual. That's why it's right to say there's a violence of the law and of laws—a violence of the police, the state, the legal system: the law which presents itself, in certain instances, as duty-bound to limit or monitor violence, can do so only by establishing, in its turn, something that isn't physical violence but is, nonetheless, the violence of constraint. This is a theme we do well to remember here, since it has been treated from the political and the cultural standpoints by thinkers like Georges Sorel and Walter Benjamin, not to mention Marx. And this can have considerable effects—being constrained by a norm may be experienced as being confronted with violence. But it is a diffuse, suppressed, civilized violence . . .

There is the violence applied to individuals' bodies. This consists at times in limiting the freedom of those bodies and we might call it carceral violence; at other times, it is bloody violence, the violence of wounding, murder, physical attacks.

Clearly, it is this latter violence that is in the spot-light at the moment on our streets ... the violence of gangsters or anarchists and even of war.

We have to draw a distinction between these different circles of violence because, in general, a kind of mechanism operates in which the response to violence of the one type is a violence of the second—extensive—type. For example, violence on the part of the state is met with bloody violence. In this way, a kind of endless system is put in place. It is part of the character of violence to be perpetual; it is self-generating . . . . As commonplace as this finding may be, how are we to break out of the round of violence?

SERS. Aren't there two meanings to the word violence—a destructive violence that points towards death and, at the same time, a drive that is combativeness, creativity and life force?

BARTHES. Even though it may seem to run counter to normal conceptions, I'm happy to make a distinction between the noun violence and the adjective violent. There are, in fact, states, forms of behaviour or choices that may be violent in a positive way. Or, rather, violent *and* positive—creative passions, creative radicalisms! But that is included in the adjective alone, when it is merely an attribute applied to some other purpose. Violence in itself appears when the attribute present in the adjective becomes essence ...

I'd also like to make three remarks. Violence poses an acute problem when it presents itself as being in the service of a cause or idea. Personally, I'm very uneasy when a doctrinal alibi is provided for violent or destructive behaviour. On this point, I'm with the sixteenth-century Calvinist Castellion when he states very simply: 'Killing a man is not defending a doctrine but killing a man.' In saying this, Sébastien Castellion took an opposing stance to Calvin of Geneva. What is good about this phrase is that it represents, I would say, the obstinacy of the letter, the moment when the letter of a statement—killing a man—doesn't kill but preserves life. To interpret that 'letter'—to say that to kill a man is to defend a doctrine—seems to me indefensible when judged with respect to life.

In the current state of the conversations and debates, one problem ought to be raised and indeed has been—the relation between violence and power. All power necessarily contains a violence. Though, given his political positions, Joseph de Maistre meant his remarks to have the opposite implications to those I see in them, he rightly said: 'Every kind of sovereignty is absolute by nature. Whether that sovereignty is vested in one person or several, and in whichever way powers are divided and organized, there will always in the last analysis be an absolute power that can do evil with impunity, which will therefore, in that sense, be despotic in the fullest sense of the term and against which there will be no other bulwark than insurrection.'[1] If we want to break with violence, we have to think in terms of non-power, which in current social terms means an absolutely marginal form of thinking. If you're against violence, you have to find your way to an ethics that is firm in its own position, outside the circle of power, and not put yourself in the situation of participating in power.

Thirdly and lastly, I ask myself a question: Can you be against violence only in part or, in other words, conditionally, recognizing exceptions? Is non-violence negotiable? This is a question I ask—and ask myself. I sense that you're constantly wanting to put certain objections to me, certain limitations, and I feel these too. But I'll answer you with a question: Can we undertake an assessment of the contents of violence, of its justifications?

There are, in fact, two ethical attitudes: either we arrogate to ourselves the right to judge the contents of violence—to rescue some of them and condemn others. This is what is generally done. Or else our bodily attitude to violence is that it's intolerable and, in that case, we reject the alibis

1 The quotation from de Maistre is from his 'Étude sur la souveraineté' [Study of Sovereignty] in Oeuvres complètes, VOL. 1 (Lyon: Emmanuel Vitte, 1891), p. 417.

and see non-violence as non-negotiable. But this latter is an excessive attitude which is adopted only in the limit-zones of personal morality.

SERS. Your answers are very pessimistic and barely offer a way out. And yet is there one?

BARTHES. I don't see current society as being on the path to resolving the problem of violence in a general way. At the level of its general organization, the world doesn't seem to offer any hope in that direction—states are increasing in number and each state is increasing its coercive force, its power. The socialist solutions to these problems seem to have no prospects whatever—they are making no headway. This is the lesson of the last fifty years and it's the source of much of our suffering. To imagine a world without violence seems utopian. And the utopia in question isn't even an entertaining one, so little does it find sustenance in our reality.

The subject living in that society is forced to fall back on individual solutions or courses of conduct.

SERS. Is that a despairing solution?

BARTHES. Not necessarily! For two hundred years we've become used, in our philosophical and political culture, to valuing very highly something which we may, in general, term collectivism.

All the philosophies are philosophies of collectiveness, of society—individualism is very much frowned upon. We no longer—or only very rarely—find philosophies of non-gregariousness and of the person. Perhaps we should actually come to terms with this singularity and not see it as somehow demeaning or shameful, but effectively re-think a philosophy of the subject [*philosophie du sujet*]; should not allow ourselves to be cowed by this morality of the collective superego with its values of political commitment and responsibility, which is diffusely present in our society. Perhaps we have to accept the scandalousness of individualistic positions, though all this requires more precise formulation.

SERS. That doesn't seem scandalous to me. Don't we first have to 'be' before 'being with'?

BARTHES. Oh, but it's a scandal for the whole of thought and theorization since, let's say, Hegel! Every philosophy that tries to sidestep these collective imperatives is extremely singular and has, I would say, a bad image.

SERS. And is that what you think too, Roland Barthes?

BARTHES. I'm trying gradually to free myself from all that's imposed on me intellectually like this. But slowly . . . You have to let the transformation take its course . . .

Réforme (2 September 1978)

Reply to a Question on Artists and Politics

This short text, republished from the magazine *Arts* of 1 December 1965, is a response to a survey on politics organized on the occasion of the presidential election in which De Gaulle was returned to the Élysee Palace after defeating François Mitterand. Alongside Barthes, respondents included the filmmaker André Cayatte and the theatre director Antoine Bourseiller. *Arts* was edited by André Parinaud and counted numerous major artists and writers among its contributors, such as François Truffaut, Jean-Luc Godard, Éric Rohmer, Jacques Laurent and Roger Nimier.

Oeuvres complètes, Volume 5, p. 1025

It seems to me that there are, in general, two ways for a writer to enter politics (the way we might talk about entering freemasonry). He can enter through the great gate of concepts and ideologies, subordinating his work to a deep-seated political choice of a Marxist or, alternatively, a liberal-humanist type, for example. Or he can enter through a much narrower gate, but one that opens on to a path that takes him further. In this latter case, his task is to take the way people talk about and do politics—and are, not infrequently, alienated by it—and find in that a set of meanings that becomes the driving force of his writing. At the moment, for example, no day goes by without my wanting, as I read the newspaper, watch a television programme or listen to a taxi driver, to transform what I'm reading or hearing into what I'll call mythological matter—that is to say, into a discourse lying somewhere between criticism and the novel.

The problems of distribution and consumption a writer may encounter have much more to do with politics than is generally thought, not only because the very economy of the literary market has political implications, but also because there are in the literary community (among both critics and consumers) styles of thinking that are ultimately political. The kinds of censorship a writer may encounter are always, when all is said and done, ideological—and hence political—in nature.

Arts (1 December 1965)